Backroads of
WASHINGTON

May 18, 1980. Mount St. Helens erupts, sending a plume of steam and volcanic ash some ten miles into the air.

MARCH 27, 1980, MOUNT ST. HELENS, whose demureness is
ribed with a great degree of enthusiasm in the Burley Mountain
ter (page 108), ended 123 years of silence with a series of spec-
lar but relatively harmless eruptions. Then on May 18, 1980, at
a.m., local time, the northwest face of the mountain exploded
such force that the 9,677-foot-high cone was transformed into a
op some 8,300 feet high.

he explosion was heard as far away as Canada, and the damage
catastrophic. A week later, a score of persons were known dead
the missing included some 70 more. A wall of mud, boulders,
and trees swept down the mountain's western slope, covering
it Lake and creating a 20-foot wall of water and debris that
ed down the Toutle River. The mud flow demolished homes,
hes, logging camps, and bridges, then surged into the Columbia
r, clogging shipping lanes. (The sketch map on page 101 shows
nt St. Helens and the area most affected by the mud slide.)

n the eastern, unpopulated slopes, the major damage was to
life and the billions of board feet of timber leveled by the blast.

50,000-foot-high cloud of ash expelled by the eruption was
n by prevailing winds to the towns, farms, and ranches of East-
Washington. As the ash settled it blotted out the sun, and many
ns were completely dark by noon on that fateful Sunday.

he cloud moved across Yakima, Ellensburg, Moses Lake, the
Cities of Richland, Pasco, and Kennewick, Walla Walla,
man, and Spokane. Hardest hit was Adams County, where
rly six inches fell on the county seat of Ritzville. By the time the

UPI

Mount St. Helens in quieter days.
In the foreground, Spirit Lake, now buried under debris
from the volcano's May 18 eruption.

Jan Fardell

cloud reached the Idaho border, it covered a 100-mile-wide sw
Interstate 90 between Ellensburg and Spokane was closed, as v
numerous smaller highways. A second eruption a week later s
tered a lighter load of ash across much of Western Washington
Northeastern Oregon.

As this is being written, in late May, 1980, only the Okanc
Highlands, the Northern Cascades, and the Puget Sound area n
of Tacoma have experienced no ash fallout. Scientists expected n
eruptions but predicted that the worst was over. The major ha.
to travelers created by the fallout is to their vehicles, for the g
fluffy ash contains enough grit to damage engines. It is believed
most highways will be open by summer, but visitors to Washin¡
should check with the State Patrol, local law enforcement agen
the AAA, or other travel clubs before planning trips into affe
areas.

Mount St. Helens can be safely viewed from a variety of place
Interstate 5 between Vancouver and Olympia, and special v
points have been established by the highway department. Vis
should not attempt to drive up the Toutle River Valley while clea
is in progress.

Backroads of
WASHINGTON

by Archie Satterfield

RAND M^cNALLY & COMPANY
CHICAGO · NEW YORK · SAN FRANCISCO

Page 1: *The Olympic Mountains*

Overleaf: *Moses Coulee*

PHOTO CREDITS

Ray Atkeson, 34, 106, 141; Asahel Curtis, courtesy the Special Collections, University of Washington, 94, 99; David Muench, 70, 123.

All black-and-white and all full-color photographs not listed above were taken by Archie Satterfield.

Sketch maps drawn by Gene Sharp, based on maps prepared by Rand McNally Cartographic Department.

The author is indebted to Hugh N. Stratford for his superb printing of all his black-and-white photographs.

Library of Congress Cataloging in Publication Data:
Satterfield, Archie.
    BACKROADS OF WASHINGTON.

        1. Washington (State)—Description and travel—
1951–   —Tours. 2. Automobiles—Road guides—
Washington (State) 3. Washington (State)—History,
Local. 4. Satterfield, Archie. I. Title.
F889.3.S28   917.97'0443   80-13251
ISBN 0-528-81101-0

First printing, 1980

Contents

Lake Crescent

Backroads of
WASHINGTON

General store at Bodie

Introduction

IN THE OLD DAYS NOT TOO MANY YEARS AGO, travel by car was accomplished at a more leisurely pace. Cars built before World War II and shortly thereafter simply wouldn't go very fast, and even if they could, most roads were built in a fashion that would send us bumping off into a farmer's field if we drove much over the present 55-mile-per-hour speed limit. Highways meandered up and down hillsides, following the contours of the earth, then abruptly turned corners instead of long, banked curves. They went around instead of across farmland. In this process of zigzagging across the countryside we had an opportunity to see the scenery. We went along so slowly that we could read the fine print on the baking-soda signs and the medical advertisements on barns. We could study the architecture of mailboxes and count the chickens in the barnyard.

Unfortunately cars and highways have been "improved" over the last quarter of a century to the point that we might as well ride a guided missile, and until the national speed limit was imposed at 55, we *were* riding guided missiles. We roared across the countryside, white-knuckled with fear, and never dared look at the scenery. This was just as well, since the Interstate System intentionally sought out the least interesting landscape all over the nation. We were extremely mobile, yet isolated. Our only contacts with other human beings were with service-station attendants, who were usually too busy to chat anyway, highway patrolmen, and too often wrecker and ambulance drivers.

Progress took most of the fun out of car travel. We became obsessed with getting there. The Interstate System gave us tunnel vision. It became a long cannon barrel through which we shot ourselves from point to point. Getting there was no fun at all, and coming back home on an Interstate, tired and anxious for familiar surroundings, was like serving a sentence.

Not far behind the 55 M.P.H. edict came the fuel shortages and higher prices, which will probably be with us from now on. Perhaps all these dampers on our addiction to vehicles will put the automobile back into its proper perspective, and going on a car trip will again be an occasion for pleasure instead of an endurance contest.

For several months while preparing this book, my family and I went on numerous car trips ranging from one day to a week or longer, avoiding the Interstates whenever possible. We visited places we hadn't seen in several years as well as many places we had never been before. We often drove 30 or 40 miles on old blacktop without seeing another car, and these backroads were frequently through beautiful areas less than an hour from cities. We drove on old highways with trees growing so thick overhead that we could hardly see the sky, and we drove on flat dirt roads past ranches and farms and between wheat fields without a sign of habitation from horizon to horizon.

There are several roads and large chunks of land that go without mention in this book, especially in some of the national forests. I tried to drive over those roads that would be safe for all and avoided some of the rougher, more primitive logging roads designed for heavy logging trucks and not for the family automobile.

Nearly all of these trips were made in our aging Honda Civic, and we avoided roads that required four-wheel-drive vehicles; after all, where can't you take them? Rock climbing?

Some of the backroads we traveled were paved, and a few, like one definition of ghost towns, were a shadow of their former selves. We traveled some that had been abandoned when the Interstates were built. Others were abandoned when the US Highway System was built before that, making them the first of three generations of highways. These highways are used only by local residents or the occasional reactionary malcontents like us.

On the subject of malcontents, some have suggested from time to time that Washington should be split into two states with the boundary following the Pacific Crest Trail along the top of the Cascade Range. The east side is agricultural, mostly treeless and flat and thinly populated; the west side is mountainous, wet, increasingly urban, and its residents generally as ignorant of Eastern Washington as of the plains of Pakistan.

I don't subscribe to this political daydream at all; if for no better reason than that the present boundaries give to Washington a greater variety of scenery

Pilchuck Creek

10

than many other states can offer. I have divided the state into three portions: Eastern Washington, the Cascade Range, and Western Washington, with some subdivisions between. Since the Cascades are in private ownership or used for logging, or in national parks and wilderness areas, there are only two areas accessible to the casual traveler. But those two areas—the Mountain Loop Highway in the central Cascades and the Mount Adams–Mount St. Helens backcountry—are gorgeous enough to keep the most imaginative writer searching for new ways to say gorgeous. I went only where there were adequate roads but blazed no new trails and challenged no logging trucks on their own turf. Nearly the entire Olympic Range is enclosed by a national park and the few roads that penetrate it are too heavily used to be called backroads. But not the Gifford Pinchot National Forest between Mount Adams and Mount St. Helens. The thought of that area almost always elicits an "ahhhh" of satisfaction from me.

Otherwise we studied maps and hoped our little car would navigate the roads. A few times we put the maps aside and just followed a road with an interesting name to see where it led. In this process of blundering off into new territories we found some excellent trips. We also found some disappointments that required backtracking several miles. Once I was totally confused and took photographs and made notes on the assumption I was one place when I really was at another, but it made a nice side trip off a main highway.

That is part of the fun of backroading; if you know what to expect on such a journey, there is really no need to take it. The best trips are those with surprises along the way or at the end. Repeatedly while traveling for this book one of the children would ask where we were. I would honestly say I didn't know, and I would give the same answer when they asked where we were going. They have said "Daddy's lost" so many times before that I didn't hear it once on this series of adventures.

I used a variety of maps for this book, including many Forest Service maps and maps of the US Geological Survey, 1:250,000 and 1:500,000 series. None are perfect, but for the sake of consistency the USGS maps were used as the basis for the sketch maps of each trip.

Whenever possible, I chose a major route between two points—an old highway between two towns, for example—then made looping side trips off it. Other routes were themselves the destinations, and only a few were less interesting than the major routes nearby.

We can't go back to rumble seats, running boards, and patent medicine signs, but we can slow down, turn off the Interstate, and explore. There is easily a year's supply of trips in this book, and by searching out your own, a lifetime could be spent exploring the state. I have been here more than 20 years and thought I knew the state well until I prepared this book. You'll find, as we did, that backroading is relaxing and puts the pleasure back into driving an automobile. You'll also learn, as I did, to be careful when telling the natives they live on a backroad. It is a relative term. What constitutes a backroad to city residents is a street, and a busy one, to the people who live along it.

So go out and explore your own set of backroads. You will never know if that road winding off the main route goes past a beautiful stream or dead-ends at a barnyard. Be brave and blunder off down some of those roads you've been driving past for years. Who knows, it may not be a dead end after all.

11

Eastern Washington

Too HERE IS A TENDENCY AMONG RESIDENTS of the western side of the Cascade Mountains to lump all of the geography east of the Cascades into one immense piece of bland real estate. It is generally referred to as East of the Mountains, or more simply Eastern Washington. That is a woefully inadequate way to describe, or dismiss, some of the most varied topography in the entire Pacific Northwest. There are at least a dozen subdivisions of this part of the state, each individual and easily distinguished from the others. These include:

The Columbia Basin: Alternately called the Big Bend area because it is enclosed on two sides by the Columbia River where it suddenly cuts south, this area now is more commonly known for the Columbia Basin Project spawned by the construction of the Grand Coulee Dam. From the dam, the water is siphoned down to Banks Lake and other holding lakes before being sent in canals to the farmlands. Originally the region was near-desert ("You had to prime yourself before you could spit," old-timers said), but the water has turned it into one of the best farming areas in the country.

The Yakima Valley: Although large vineyards, hops farms, and row crops have long been established in the Yakima River Valley, this area, as well as the

Facing page:
Switchbacks
on Washington 126
coming out of
Tucannon River
Valley

13

Wenatchee Hills to the north, has long been known nationally as apple country. It is inconceivable to state residents that anyone could drive through this area during the summer months without stopping at roadside fruit stands to stock up on apples, pears, peaches, apricots, and various vegetables.

The Dry-Land Wheat-Farming Area: This takes in most of the central portion of Eastern Washington, south from Roosevelt Lake to the Tri-Cities of Richland, Pasco, and Kennewick, and east from the irrigated land of the Columbia Basin to the Palouse Hills. Rainfall here is just a fraction above that in a desert climate, but enough to grow wheat crops without irrigation. Nevertheless, irrigation is slowly working its way into the area, giving farmers higher yields and a wider selection of crops to grow.

The Horse Heaven Hills: These barren and broken hills are between the Columbia River on the south and the Yakima Valley on the north. Some irrigated crops are grown in the hills, watered mostly by wells, but the region still retains an open-range atmosphere and supports only a small population of ranchers and farmers.

The Snake River Canyon: This area runs west from the good wheat and row-crop farming area around Walla Walla and Dayton on east to the Idaho border. It is against the northern edge of the Blue Mountains in Umatilla National Forest, and runs north to the Snake River. Like the Horse Heaven Hills, much of this area is too steep and broken for good farming, so you're more likely to see ranches than crops.

The Palouse: A rich wheat-farming region that is described in a separate chapter; it runs north from the Snake River to the Spokane Valley.

The Channeled Scabland: A series of canyons that is roughly the western border of the Palouse, also described in another chapter.

Okanogan Highlands: This is another indistinct geographic subdivision, but includes the area east of the Cascades and north of the Columbia River toward the Idaho border.

Kettle River Range: This is a small range in the central part of Northern Washington, a series of ridges running north and south in the Republic area.

The Selkirk Mountains: This chain comes out of Idaho and into Washington along the Pend Oreille River north of Newport.

Much of Eastern Washington was settled by farm and cattle and sheep people. Only in the Okanogan Hills was gold a major factor in creating towns and communities, and many of these are long since abandoned. But most of the towns there were built to last, and the small towns of Eastern Washington will often have substantial homes built around the turn of the century, sometimes before. The whole area has a look of permanence to it.

In almost every way, Eastern Washington simply looks different from the rest of the state. It is desert and hill country, with annual rainfall ranging from less than ten inches a year to perhaps double that. Some places in Eastern Washington get no more rain in 15 years than the Olympic coastal towns of Queets and La Push receive in a single year.

Facing page:
A tattered windmill

14

GOLDENDALE TO MABTON

IF YOU LIKE YOUR SPACES wide open and unpopulated, this long drive from Goldendale to the Yakima Valley will make your vacation. I didn't know what to expect when I took the turn in Goldendale toward Bickleton but assumed I would see some beautiful rolling landscape. I wasn't disappointed.

Goldendale itself is a pleasant farming community with enough elevation to have timber, close enough to the Columbia River and the Mount Adams backcountry to have lakes and streams nearby for fishing and boating. It has an excellent county museum and several Victorian-era homes and public buildings in good condition. A small observatory is on a hill outside of town, and when an eclipse is scheduled for the Northwest, thousands of people flock to the hillsides and farms to camp overnight and watch the show.

The road to Bickleton and Mabton begins climbing immediately after leaving Goldendale and levels off on top of a plateau. Oak trees grow in the canyons and the gullies off the road, and I found a sunflower farm not too far along the route.

For the most part, the road travels through unpopulated country. It is paved until it reaches a stretch of broken land and drops down into Badger Gulch, where a series of creeks, dry so far as I could tell, merge to become Rock Creek. After the road winds down into the gulch then back up on top again, the pavement returns.

The first community of any size is Cleveland, which was settled in 1879 by a man from that Ohio city. It has a rather grand cemetery near the road and a cluster of houses. Just a short distance along the road is the only real town in the area, Bickleton. Here you will find a small, one-story store with an oversized false front; the whole thing is painted a rather striking bright green. There are a grocery store, tavern, and the other businesses typical of small farm and ranch towns. Bickleton was settled the same year as Cleveland by a man named Bickle, who used to deliver the mail between his home and Goldendale, a two-day horseback trip each way.

The road continues through ranches and occasional farms beyond Bickleton. Then, dramatically, it drops over the crest of a steep hill and there laid out before you is the Yakima Valley, green and inviting after the dry drive. The road curves and switchbacks its way to the valley floor, then makes a straight run toward the small town of Mabton.

*Badger Gulch
on Rock Creek*

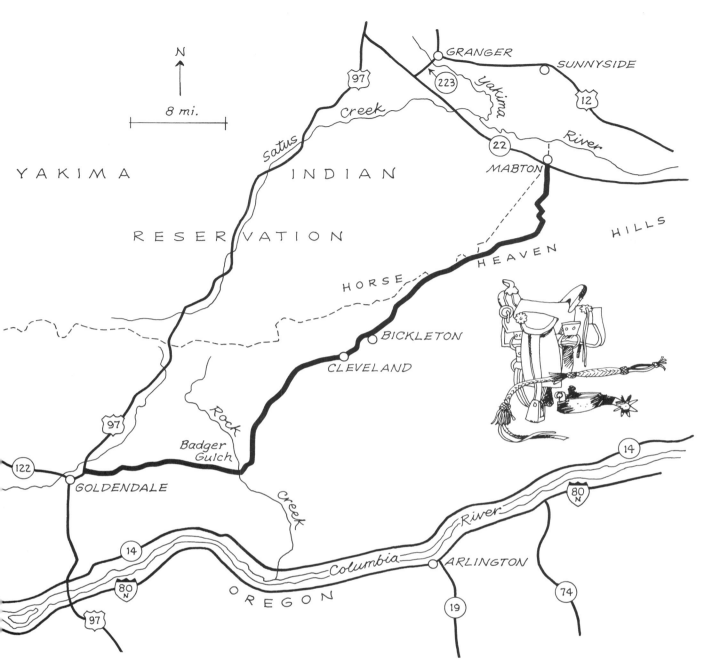

YAKIMA

INDIAN

RESERVATION

N

8 mi.

Satus Creek

97

223

yakima

GRANGER

SUNNYSIDE

12

22

MABTON

River

HORSE

HEAVEN

HILLS

BICKLETON

CLEVELAND

Rock

97

Badger Gulch

122

GOLDENDALE

Creek

14

80 N

River

14

80 N

Columbia

ARLINGTON

97

OREGON

19

74

*Sunflower farm
near Goldendale*

17

*Rodin sculpture
in Maryhill Museum*

Washington Sketch:
MARYHILL MUSEUM

FIRST-TIME VISITORS to Maryhill Museum are always amazed to find such an imposing structure, a mansion of grand proportions, out in the middle of the sagebrush and jumbled lava overlooking the Columbia River more than 100 miles from any major population center. Even more surprising are some of the museum's treasures: many gifts from the Queen of Rumania and dozens of statues by the sculptor Rodin.

But the museum dates back to an era before income taxes when millionaires were very, instead of modestly, wealthy. If they felt a whim coming on, they could cater to it.

Samuel Hill, a Seattle attorney who had his own millions, had married the daughter of the railroad tycoon James J. Hill, thus saving her the trouble of changing her last name. Between the two was a great deal of money that obviously had to be spent for something. Hill wanted a palatial country place. Although it might never match William Randolph Hearst's San Simeon castle, he could afford one as handsome as any in Washington.

He sent a crew of men out to scour the state for a suitable location, remote and striking, and they came back with the site south of Goldendale on the Columbia River, a barren and windy place with no other structures in sight. Hill was delighted with it and bought as much land around the area as he could. Construction began in 1914, with one hitch; his wife, Mary, hated the place without ever seeing it, and apparently never did see it. Eventually they separated.

But Hill persisted and kept construction going along rather fitfully during World War I. After the war he served on the Hoover Commission to help restore the war-torn European nations, including Rumania. During this period he met three women who were to have an impact on his country place: Queen Marie of Rumania and an American dancer named Loie Fuller, who by this time was living in semiretirement in Paris after having been one of the most popular dancers of all time in the Folies Bergère. The third was Alma de Bretteville Spreckles, the Los Angeles art patron of the sugar family.

Hill's plans for his estate in the sagebrush kept changing. He first named it Promised Land, then changed it to Marylands, then Maryhill to honor both his wife and daughter. He laid out plans for a Quaker colony on the land and built them a meeting hall, a hotel, and a business office. The Quakers liked it no better than Hill's wife, and refused to live there.

Construction dragged along until Loie Fuller suggested that the mansion be used as a museum, and then Hill's interest revived. The building was provided with large rooms suitable for museum exhibits, and Hill and Loie prevailed upon Queen Marie to visit America and dedicate the museum. This she did, in 1926, traveling across the country in a train and hounded by newspapermen skeptical of her intentions. She brought with her numerous trappings of royalty from her own collection, including thrones, clothing, tapestries, and artwork, and these she donated to Hill.

But due to Hill's on-again, off-again interest the museum wasn't completed at his death in 1931. His ashes were placed in a tomb he had ordered built in the

19

canyon wall beneath the imposing structure. It wasn't until 1940 that the museum was opened to the public. Another of his friends, Alma de Bretteville Spreckles, took over, donated an undisclosed sum to have the mansion readied for opening, and donated some pieces from her own vast art collection for the occasion. The remainder of the collection, which we see today, consists of Hill's own collection and those pieces donated by the Queen of Rumania.

Hill also built a replica of Stonehenge on a hill east of the museum to honor the World War I dead of Klickitat County, and he erected the giant Peace Arch on the US–Canadian border at Blaine.

Unfortunately, with the passage of time, his more famous father-in-law, James J. Hill, has mistakenly received credit for the other Hill's efforts. It is unknown if he is responsible for the exclamatory question that has lodged itself in our language—"What in Sam Hill?" We do know, however, that Jim Hill mustard, a noxious and prolific weed, was named for James J. Hill because his Great Northern Railroad was accused of importing it to the Northwest.

WASHINGTON HIGHWAY 126

IF, ON THIS ROUTE, you find yourself in a series of steep switchbacks that you think you can't negotiate with your car, don't say you weren't warned.

When Washington Highway 126 peels off the major Southeastern Washington route of US Highway 12, there are at least two warning signs telling you the road is not recommended for through traffic and that cars pulling trailers should try another way. If the weather is foul, you should probably skip the drive for the time being.

The pretty trip begins six miles north of the vegetable-canning town of Dayton. The road runs down a shallow draw between farms and past an occasional grain elevator, looking quite innocent in the process. Then you come to a sign that tells you the road is dirt for the next seven miles. That's where the fun begins. The highway builders selected one of the depressions heading down toward the Tucannon River for a roadbed. The road gets progressively steeper until it emerges in a cluster of houses and barns named Marengo. After crossing a road that runs on up the Tucannon River, Highway 126 starts switchbacking its way up the eastern side of the canyon. The road surface here is no easier to drive on than loose marbles, but once above the canyon it is smooth driving on pavement again. It is a short distance on in to US 12 just west of Pomeroy.

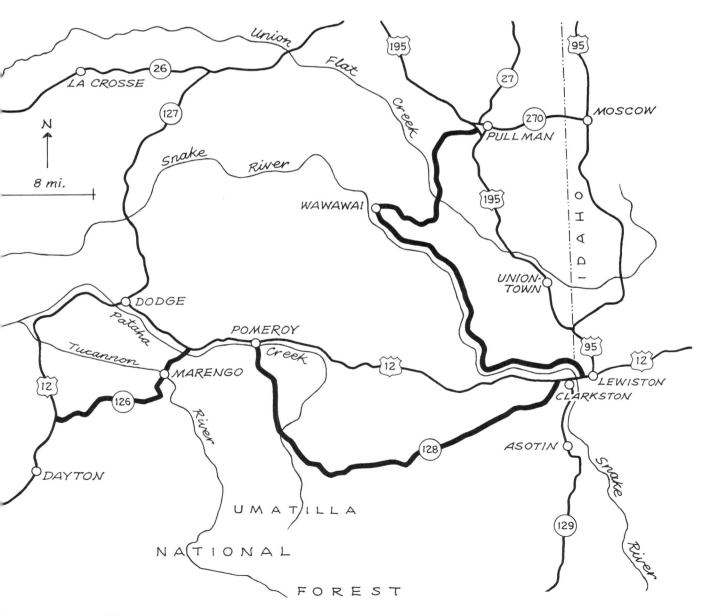

Right: Grain elevator on Washington 126

Facing page: Old stagecoach depot, Dayton

WASHINGTON HIGHWAY 128

I STARTED OUT on Highway 128 from Pomeroy intending to explore the heart of the Blue Mountains. Previously I had stuck to the main roads that go through this forest of pine and had decided that this time I would go all the way through from Pomeroy to the Grand Ronde River, then back up to Anatone and Clarkston.

This plan was quickly abandoned. Each time I tried one of the Forest Service roads that led to the south, I began fearing for the little Honda's life. On one narrow road I almost became intimately acquainted with the grill of a logging truck. So I went back to Highway 128 and stayed there. Maybe another time I'll make it, but not this year.

Yet I don't feel cheated of scenery because Highway 128 goes to the edge of the mountains and gives you a selection of scenery ranging from wheat farms to ranches to the forests on the edge of the Blue Mountains in Umatilla National Forest. It makes no pretense of being a modern, flat highway, and occasionally you'll find yourself descending a steep hill on a gravel road that goes right through the front yard of a farm or ranch.

The whole route is very scenic. Some of my favorite views are along the last half, which I traveled late in the afternoon. After the route leaves the wooded hills it goes along several miles of very steep, barren ridges too dry for timber and too steep for crops. These sharp, sculpted hillsides look like modern paintings when the sun hits them from a low angle and catches the subtle colors that are always there in combinations that change with the season, from several shades of green in the spring to browns in the autumn.

The best of this barren scenery appears in the last few miles. First you pass a ranch with an unusual octagonal barn just below the road; originally it was a dance hall for ranchers and farmers back in the hills. You climb a bit more to the top of the plateau just in time to start down again with the whole Snake River Valley laid out before you, from beyond Lewiston and Clarkston on the east to several miles of the valley on the west. This is one of the highest points in the area, and if you arrive on top on a clear day, you will encounter a sight you will remember for years.

The highway ends on the western edge of Clarkston, where you rejoin US Highway 12.

Facing page: *Eroded hills above Clarkston on Washington 128*

Below: *Rod weeder and hitch*

Dr. Marcus Whitman

Narcissa Whitman

Washington Sketch:
THE WHITMANS

UNTIL RECENTLY, historians have written of the Whitmans' death as a massacre, but when an Indian history of the Northwest is written, the incident at Waiilatpu, "place of the rye grass," most probably will be labeled in a different fashion.

Medical missionary Marcus Whitman brought his bride, Narcissa, across the Oregon Trail in 1836 to open a mission near Fort Walla Walla in the Oregon Territory. In 1837, a daughter, Alice Clarissa, was born on Narcissa's 29th birthday. (She was the first white child born west of the Rockies and north of California.) Some of the religious fire went from the parents' lives when the little girl was drowned on Sunday, June 23, 1839, while getting a cup of water from the Walla Walla River.

The Whitmans stayed on, preaching to the Indians, treating those who were ill, and helping the few overlanders who came by on their way to the Willamette Valley at the end of the Oregon Trail.

Marcus Whitman was a tough, demanding missionary. There were stories about his methods of converting the Indians, and working them in the fields. Apparently he didn't hesitate to punish them with the rod, since he always insisted they were like children. He tried to force them to learn white man's ways and religion, but he learned very little of the Indians' own culture. He probably would have been surprised if someone suggested they even had a culture.

Whitman built a small, self-sustaining village. There was a millpond for a grist mill, and he used some of the water to irrigate 40 acres of farmland and a 75-tree orchard. There was a blacksmith shop and also a rough hotel-like structure for travelers, which he called the Emigrant House.

By 1847, the Whitmans had been at Waiilatpu 11 years, but their influence over the spiritual lives of the local Cayuse Indians was not strong. Nevertheless Whitman and Narcissa remained, building, cultivating, preaching, and tending to the ill. Had Whitman only studied the Indians' beliefs, he and Narcissa and 11 other mission residents might have died of natural causes.

That year the Cayuse suffered from an outbreak of measles, and many died. Whitman's medicine seemed to have no effect, and the Indians came to believe his medicine was in fact killing them. Even had this suspicion not existed, the Indians' custom was to kill medicine men whose cures no longer worked.

On November 29, 1847, a Cayuse chief, Tomahas, came into the mission shrouded in a blanket, complaining of illness. Whitman stepped forward to help him. Tomahas pulled a tomahawk from beneath the blanket and struck Whitman. Other Cayuse came into the mission, and when they were through with the attack, 13 whites, including Marcus and Narcissa, lay dead in the compound.

The mission was never reopened, but in 1881 the Oregon Pioneer Historical Society was given eight acres of its land. Congress designated Whitman Mission a national memorial in 1936, and it became a national historic site in 1963; it has been maintained by the National Park Service since. Archaeological work continues on the site and many artifacts from the Whitman years are on exhibit.

27

*Snake River Canyon
near Wawawai*

28

WAWAWAI

THIS ROUTE, which is difficult to pronounce without giving or taking a "wah," takes you right down into the Snake River Canyon from the twin cities of Lewiston and Clarkston. Unfortunately (from the tourist's standpoint), the treacherous river is all slack water along here now, but the serrated and layered cliffs remain.

When I drove the route, the new bridge at Clarkston wasn't quite completed. I had to sneak across the river into Lewiston, Idaho, drive a short distance north, then turn left off US Highway 195 on Front Street while looking for a sign aiming me toward Wilma, which isn't a town but a Port of Clarkston railroad- and barge-loading area.

Before the dams were completed, the Snake was wild river. The first white men to make the run down it to the Columbia River were members of the Lewis and Clark Expedition, guided by the friendly Nez Perce Indians who lived in the Snake River area. The Lewis and Clark party was quite weak by this time. Not long before they had almost starved while crossing the Bitterroot Range in deep snow, and when the Nez Perce gave them dried, and sometimes rather ripe, salmon, their stomachs rebelled. Some of the men ran the rapids of the Snake too weak to walk. Although the river was very swift then, the party had to spend so much time portaging around the worst rapids, and plucking each other out of the river, that they made very poor time.

The first settlers in the canyon came before the turn of this century, and most began as ranchers. Then they found it was possible to grow fine orchards in the canyon, and for decades it was a tradition to go down to the Snake and pick your own fruit. At first, the major transportation into the canyon was by steamboat, but a spur of a railroad was built along the narrow banks in 1908 between Riparia and Lewiston. Soon it was followed by a rough road for horse-drawn vehicles, then for automobiles.

Wheat farmers on the plateaus high above the Snake built chutes and tramways to move their grain down to barges that traveled on the river. Remains of a few of these can be seen at various points along the riverbanks.

A trip to Wawawai and out of the canyon is tame now when you consider the canyon's past, but the trip is still a beautiful one and much more interesting than following the herd along Highway 195 between Lewiston and Pullman. After the Lower Granite Dam flooded the canyon to a depth of 80 feet in 1974, the Corps of Engineers built a new shelf for the railroad and highway. At first you think you're going to travel the whole route with the railroad between you and the river, but the paved highway and railroad soon switch sides, and the highway has frequent turnouts where you can park to stretch your legs. There is also an occasional camping and boat-launching area.

Unfortunately, all the orchards along the canyon are under water now.

This trip provides a short course in the state's geological history. You can see successive fissure lava flows layered along the canyon walls, and an occasional intrusion of granite and other older forms of stone. The canyon walls change colors depending on lighting conditions and the time of day.

Since there is nothing to be gained by lamenting the passage of the wild waters of the canyon, you might as well enjoy what it has to offer today. One of the prettiest sights you'll see now is a towboat with a barge coming up the narrow canyon on a calm day, matched by their reflections in the water.

The road takes a sharp turn to the right at Wawawai and heads through a narrow, V-shaped canyon back up to the wheat plateau. After crossing Highway 195, it takes you into Pullman.

Steptoe Butte
from hill overlooking
Palouse River
and Elberton

THE PALOUSE COUNTRY

NOBODY IS ABSOLUTELY CERTAIN what the word "Palouse" means. It was picked up from the local Indians, who called themselves the Palouse but didn't seem to know why. The Palouse Country has no distinct boundaries, like similar areas that are distinct from other geographical locations in the middle but become fuzzy on the edges. Generally speaking, the Palouse runs north from the Snake River to the Spokane River Valley, west into the Channeled Scabland, and east up against forests in Idaho.

Most of the Palouse consists of rolling, low hills with loess, wind-blown soil, up to 100 feet deep. The rich land combined with the elevation and the resulting increased rainfall makes the Palouse Country the best wheat-growing area in the nation, and some say in the entire world. This rise in elevation is virtually impossible to detect as you drive across Eastern Washington, but within less than 50 miles the wheat production on unirrigated land increases 20 to 30 bushels per acre. The weather is also on the side of the Palouse. Whereas the Great Plains and Montana suffer from droughts, blizzards, freezing weather, hail storms, tornadoes, and other afflictions, the Palouse, as well as the neighboring dry-land wheat-farming areas, seldom has severe crop losses from the weather.

When the first settlers arrived in the mid-19th century, most coming by wagon from Walla Walla, they had no idea they were staking claims on such rich land. The rolling hills were covered with bunchgrass then, and most timber for lumber was brought in from Idaho. But apparently somebody planted wheat early on, and that started the industry. A jealous dry-land farmer once said that all the Palouse farmers have to do is stick the seed wheat in the ground, then jump back and run before they get lost in the jungle of grain.

When the first mobile combines were built to thresh grain, the steep hills of the Pa-

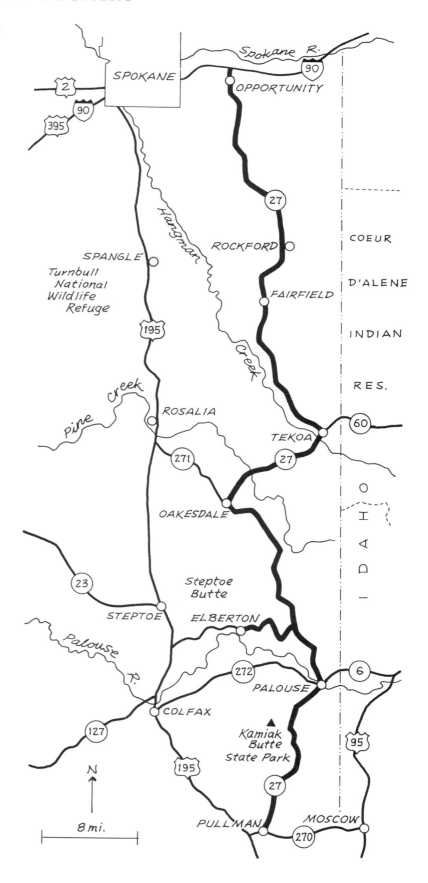

louse created problems that at first appeared impossible to solve. In order for combines to work properly, the machinery that separates grain from the stalk must remain level at all times. Otherwise, grain will be lost or mixed with so much chaff that it won't really be separated.

A family of mechanics and inventors in the town of Palouse came up with the solution. They invented an attachment triggered by a mercury switch, which jacked one side or other of the combine up and down automatically. This made combines look like they were traveling on one stilt as they went along steep hillsides, but it kept the separator mechanism level and paid for itself before the first harvest was over.

The best time to drive through the Palouse Country is in the spring when everything is green, or late August and early September toward the end of harvest. And the best time of day is early or late, when the sun creates shadows along the hills to define them more clearly and create interesting designs.

My favorite trip through the hills is Washington Highway 27, which starts at Pullman and ends at Opportunity, just east of Spokane. It is slower and much more crooked than the newer US Highway 195, but since traffic is lighter, you won't be terrified of stopping on the shoulder to absorb a scene or take a picture.

The first town out of Pullman is Palouse, with lots of brick buildings and old houses that reflect several generations of ownership. But before you reach Palouse, there is one short side trip worth the time, over to Kamiak Butte State Park. The 3,360-foot butte has a county park on its wooded summit and a hiking trail along the highest ridge for more views of the countryside. Again, a reminder that early or late in the day is best, not only because of the shadow effect that delineates the terrain but also because at midday there is sometimes a haze or dust in the air that obscures the scenery.

The butte was named for Kamiakin, the Yakima Indian chief who was so effective an enemy of the whites, particularly Colonel Steptoe. (See the historical sketch on the Steptoe Campaign.)

You will notice a nice touch by early highway builders and town planners as you enter towns along Highway 27. There are always speed-limit signs outside town, then just as you enter town the highway makes a sudden sharp turn, almost a corner, before entering the main street. If the signs don't slow you down, the sharp corner will. This trick is apparent in nearly every town on this route.

A short distance north of Palouse is a county road leading off to the west marked "Elberton." Go there. It is one of the few towns in the Palouse that have virtually rolled up their sidewalks. Elberton started as a sawmilling town on the Palouse River, but the pine and fir trees along the river didn't last long. Then a fruit drier was built there, believed to have been the largest such plant of its kind. But the area isn't a major fruit producer, either. Gradually people moved out of Elberton until only a half dozen or so families were left in town or living on the hills surrounding it.

Students at Washington State University in Pullman 30 miles away became interested in Elberton and drew up plans to turn it into a lived-in county park. The general store, the community church, and the post office built in 1877 would be preserved under the students' plans. On my last visit, the store was still open and displayed a great collection of advertisements dating back to pre–World War II days as well as many tools and decorations of the same era.

Another good side trip is from Oakesdale down to Steptoe Butte. In fact, I'm known in some circles as a nut on Steptoe Butte, and a friend who works for the Washington State Wheat Commission invariably greets me with the question: "How are things on Steptoe?" Fine, I tell him, if they'd just get those radio antennas and microwave towers off its summit.

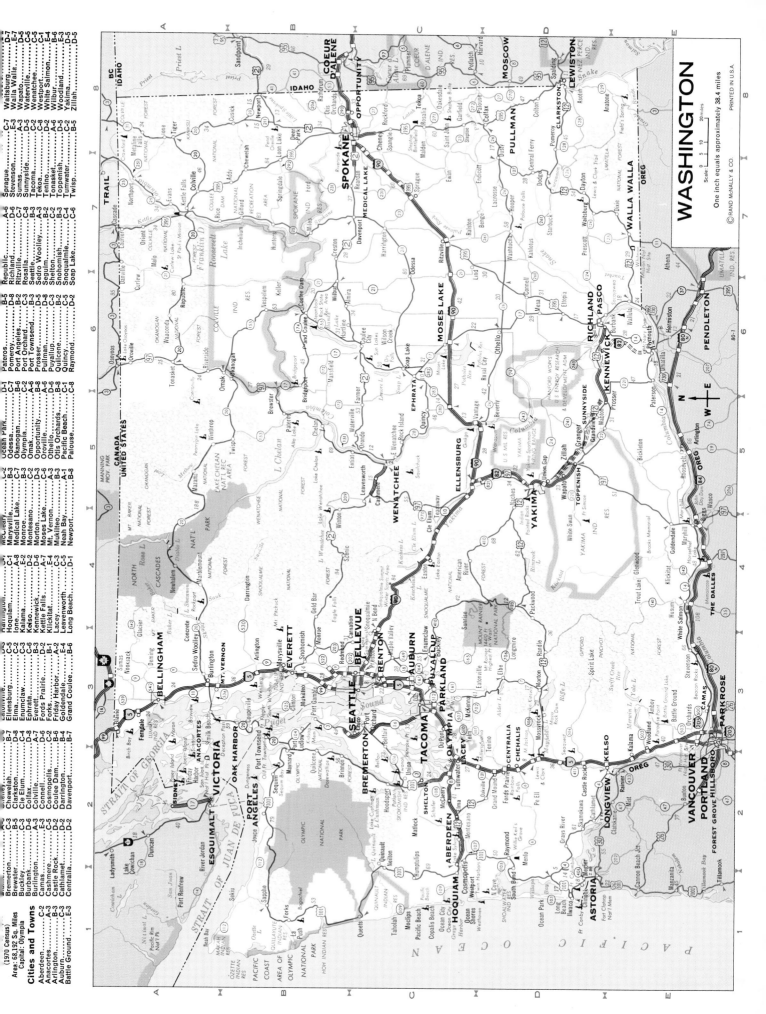

WASHINGTON

Scale:
One inch equals approximately 38.4 miles

0   5   10   20 miles

© RAND McNALLY & CO.   PRINTED IN U.S.A.

*View west
from Steptoe Butte*

As an aside, the butte has nothing to do with the Steptoe battle. It was called Pyramid Peak in those early days and didn't receive its present name until long after the Indian Wars were over.

Originally the butte was the top of a mountain, probably the tallest in a chain that led west from the Selkirk Mountains of Northern Idaho. But the rest of the mountains were buried beneath numerous lava flows that came from fissures in the earth instead of volcanoes. Then the wind-borne dirt gradually covered the lava flows, and much of Steptoe Butte. Geologists studying the area discovered that the butte was of granitic origin, and the word "steptoe" entered geological vocabularies to describe a protrusion of an older formation above newer materials.

The butte was famous around the turn of this century for the hotel that was built atop it by one of those Victorian Englishmen who seemed to pop up all over the planet. His name was James Davis, born in Sussex County, England, in 1815. He came to America in 1840 and arrived in the Palouse Country in 1872 after trying several other parts of this country and making a lot of money. At the age of 60, with a substantial ten-room house for his large family and an already successful cattle ranch, Davis got itchy feet and sold everything. He loaded up his family and headed for Canada.

But his wife had her own ideas of what the family should do, and after only one day en route to British Columbia, she called a halt to the migration. Davis listened when she spoke firmly. They set up housekeeping at a place called Cottonwood Springs, where the town of Cashup now stands. The town's name resulted from Davis's method of doing business. When he built his second ten-room house, he included a general store and an inn for the stage route that went through. His slogan for doing business was "cash up front, no credit," and he became known as Cashup Davis.

As usual, the Davis family prospered, and he looked for other investments. His eye lighted on the nearby butte protruding up with a commanding view of the whole area. Davis decided to build a first-class hotel on the summit as a stop for tourists riding the trains he believed would come by when the railroads were built. He had the magnificent wooden hotel built, but few of the anticipated trains came. However, it was very popular for locals and nearly all pioneer reminiscences of the period mention going to dances at the hotel. But its popularity with overnight guests lasted only a short time, and it became a relic before its boards were seasoned.

The hotel was Davis's major source of pride, and when he was in his 80s, he prepared for his death by digging his own grave near the hotel and telling everyone he wanted to be buried there. When he died he was on an outing to the butte to poison some ground squirrels threatening to take over the hotel. As is often the case, the living did not heed the wishes of the deceased. Davis was buried in the Steptoe cemetery in 1896. The hotel stood in ruins until 1911, when two boys set it afire. Now the butte is a state park with its summit decorated by the maze of antennas and towers.

As you drive north on Highway 27 through Tekoa, Fairfield, and Rockford, you will note that the timber gets thicker and thicker, evidence of the increase in annual rainfall, until you reach the Spokane River Valley at Opportunity. Somewhere along here—it is impossible to say just where—the Palouse Country ends.

Colonel Edward Steptoe

Washington Sketch:
THE STEPTOE CAMPAIGN

IN 1858, eighteen years before the Custer disaster at Little Big Horn, Washington Territory was almost the scene of an equally resounding victory by the Indians against the encroaching whites. On this occasion, the man in charge of the ill-fated Army expedition was Colonel Edward J. Steptoe, who left his name on the battlefield, on a small town, and on a pyramid-shaped peak nearby called Steptoe Butte.

Steptoe was the commanding officer of Fort Walla Walla, but his sympathies were with the Indians whom the territorial governor, Isaac Stevens, had been badgering, bullying, and virtually forcing to sign treaties that the Indians did not really understand. Like most Army career officers, Steptoe knew the Indians were being treated unfairly, yet he was charged with the safety of civilians who were coming into Washington Territory, particularly into what is now Idaho, in increasing numbers to seek gold.

During the two years of Stevens's treaty efforts, a Yakima chief, Kamiakin, had been making the rounds among all Indians from the Snake River north spreading the message that the Indians should evict the white settlers before they became too numerous. Adding to the Indians' resentment was the construction of a road between Fort Walla Walla and Fort Benton, the head of navigation on the Missouri River over in Montana. Although the road never amounted to much, still it represented an intrusion along a 1,000-mile route into the Indians' territory. More and more rumors of an impending Indian uprising, and reports of a few killings, filtered back to Fort Walla Walla and forced Steptoe to take action.

Much of the unrest was reported in the area of present-day Colville, and the Palouse Indians, who were near enough Fort Walla Walla for Steptoe to know they weren't docile, had been helping Kamiakin spread the uprising fever.

In May, 1858, Steptoe decided to make an expedition into the Spokane Indians' territory to discuss treaties that had been signed by the Indians and Stevens but were not yet ratified by the Senate. Steptoe organized a troop of 152 enlisted men, six officers, and a few Nez Perce scouts. All were mounted, and an additional 100 packhorses were in the train.

It was the contents of the packs carried by the horses that caused Steptoe's serious troubles. The chief packer, who later admitted his mistake, loaded the packs with food and camping equipment but no ammunition. The only ammunition was on the men's belts. Steptoe was not aware of this until the fighting began, and he was ultimately blamed for not knowing the contents of his field equipment.

He thought it would be a leisurely trek. Only the Palouse Indians were unfriendly, and Steptoe wanted to meet with them early in the trip to apprehend the murderers of two miners. But the Palouse withdrew from the Snake River and preceded Steptoe's troops north, joining with the Spokane and Coeur d'Alene tribes to build their forces. Kamiakin was there, organizing the tribes into a war machine.

They met on May 15, 1858, when Steptoe camped on Pine Creek near present-day Rosalia. The Indians set up an ambush in a gulch and waited for the troops to enter it. Scouts saw them and Steptoe detoured around the gulch, and camped that night at a small lake. The Indians later told historians the only thing that saved him from being attacked that day was the fact that it was Sunday, which reflected some of the religious teachings the Indians had been exposed to in missions in the area.

Only after a battle seemed certain did Steptoe discover the ammunition situation, and he ordered a retreat for the following morning. A scout was sent ahead to get reinforcements from Fort Walla Walla to meet Steptoe's forces at the Snake River Crossing. Steptoe believed he could outrun the Indians to the river, but the crossing itself was an excellent place for ambushes.

The soldiers had traveled only about five miles when the Indians attacked. A chief was called into a meeting by the missionary, Father Joset, who had dashed over from the Cataldo Mission in Idaho. The chief, called Vincent, was insulted and slapped by a Nez Perce scout. The battle began.

The soldiers had no water, precious little ammunition, and their guns weren't as modern as those the Indians had purchased from the Hudson's Bay Company in Canada. Nor were they carrying their cutlasses, and there was much hand-to-hand combat. The running battle continued on and off all day and until nightfall, when it was the Indians' turn to make a mistake. They believed the soldiers would be easy prey the following day, and backed off to celebrate the day's fighting and to divide the spoils from the packhorses they had managed to capture.

37

During the night Steptoe organized his escape. He sent scouts south to see if they could get through the Indians' lines, and the scouts returned without seeing any of the hostile Indians. The soldiers piled their baggage in plain sight on the hill where they had stopped, buried their dead along with the few virtually useless field howitzers, and led horses back and forth over the fresh earth to disguise the graves. They converted some of the packhorses into mounts to replace the 30-odd that had been shot out from under the troopers. They put blankets over all white horses and did what they could to pad the metal parts of harnesses and saddles that might clink and rattle. They accomplished all this within two hours after the fighting ceased, and then they divided into two groups and began sneaking off into the night.

Steptoe led the hungry, thirsty, and tired troops south to the Palouse River, where they took a brief rest and had their first drinking water in two days. They lashed the wounded into their saddles, and eventually had to abandon two men while they were still alive because the men preferred being left behind to the agony of riding. Both had worked loose from the lashings and fallen from their horses.

After a ride of 25 hours with virtually no rest, the weary troops arrived at the Snake River early in the morning and managed to cross it without loss of men or horses, aided by a group of Nez Perce camped nearby. Late that morning the reinforcements arrived from Fort Walla Walla, indicating that the scout sent ahead had made the harrowing trip of more than 100 miles in less than 36 hours, certainly one of the hardest rides in Washington's history.

Colonel Steptoe was ruined by the incident, despite his brilliant retreat. The matter of the overlooked ammunition was his downfall. He died in disgrace (at least in his own mind) in 1865.

The end of this Indian uprising came shortly after Steptoe's defeat. Colonel George Wright was sent out to put an end to the hostilities, and he pursued his mission with exceptional vigor. He followed the scorched-earth policy of killing as many Indians as he could find, destroying their villages and supplies, and hanging their chiefs. Moreover, he came to enjoy it.

Wright's most effective act probably was one that he did not completely appreciate himself until well afterward. When his troops managed to capture some 700 head of horses, Colonel Wright ordered the animals all shot. The Indians were demoralized by this cold-blooded destruction of the universal sign of wealth, and it was an act totally foreign to their way of thinking. Horses were to be stolen, but never killed.

In Wright's report, he wrote: "The chastisement which these Indians have received has been severe but well merited, and absolutely necessary to impress them with our power. For the last 80 miles our route has been marked by slaughter and devastation; 900 horses and a large number of cattle have been killed or appropriated to our own use; many houses, with large quantities of wheat and oats, also many caches of vegetables, kamas [camas], and dried berries, have been destroyed. A blow has been struck which they will never forget."

This may have been the most destructive such raid in the history of Indian warfare, but since the area was so remote from the rest of the nation at that time, little notice was taken of the expeditions then, or since.

MOSES COULEE

A FEW YEARS AGO a friend who lives near Mansfield told us about a farmer down in Moses Coulee who had strung aerial irrigation sprinklers across the coulee, from wall to wall so to speak, and how it was a popular rainy day, or Sunday afternoon, outing for farmers from all over the Big Bend area to go down and look at the sprinkler system. I had long been intrigued by Moses Coulee but had never visited it, unless you count the crossing US Highway 2 makes, which is a sudden drop in elevation, a few quick

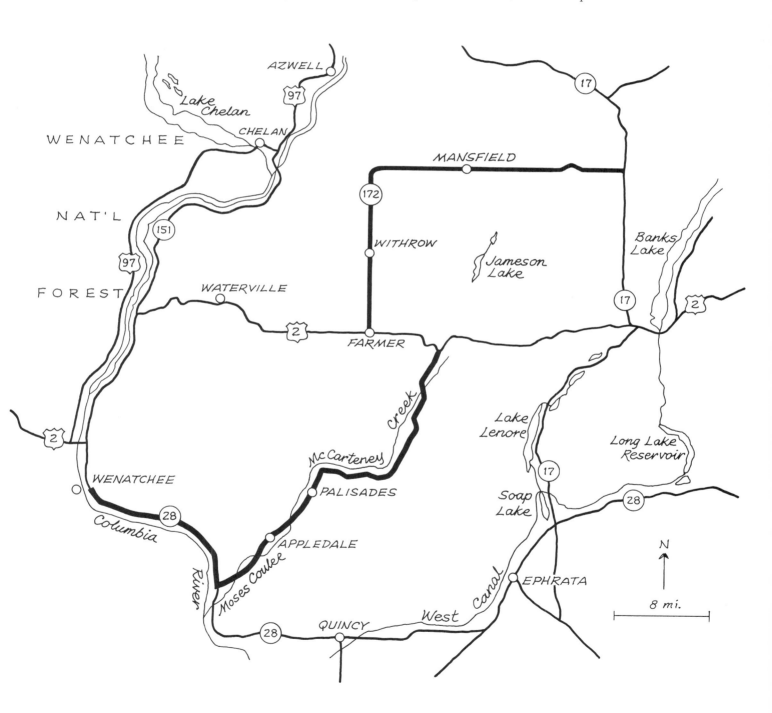

curves, and back uphill again to the wheat plateau.

Moses Coulee was one of the waterways the Columbia River used during the Ice Ages, when the Columbia was blocked by ice and debris. The river cut a series of new channels, the major one being over Dry Falls, now a state park that is across the ridge and down in the next coulee to the east. Moses Coulee was named for a popular chief of a small band of Indians who lived around Moses Lake (another namesake for him) and Waterville. Until recently there were grandparents all over the area who remembered Moses and his band.

We decided to follow it from its end up toward its beginning, and drove south from Wenatchee on Washington Highway 28, following the Columbia River past the Rock Island Dam and along a cut slightly above the river. Our map gave no number to the county road that goes up Moses Coulee, and we knew that the two towns in the coulee, Appledale and Palisades, weren't very large. As we drove along the Columbia for several miles, we began getting nervous: Have we passed the turnoff? How do we know when we do see it?

But our anxieties were soothed when we found a small sign at the bottom of a long grade pointing us toward Palisades. We turned on the narrow but paved road, and headed northeast up the flat coulee floor. The road runs along uneventfully for a few miles before it comes close to the west wall, where you can see the crumbling basalt that each year adds a bit more debris to the coulee floor through a freezing and thawing action that chips off bits and pieces, and sometimes boulders. One section of wall was strangely pocked as if attacked by a demented woodpecker.

This whole coulee region, called Coulee Country by some, was the scene of vast lava flows pouring from fissures in the earth instead of the more potent and spectacular volcanoes. After the flows ceased, the instruments of erosion—wind, weather, and water—began gradually tearing down the palisades of basalt and washing away the loose material between the lava flows. Then the wind, a steady stream of air usually out of the southwest, began blowing dirt in from Southern Washington and Oregon to create a rich loess that needed only rainfall to make it into a garden.

There is still virtually no rainfall in the coulees, but irrigation has taken care of that.

We drove past Appledale—a few houses built closer together than usual—and continued on up the gradually narrowing coulee. We went through Palisades, a small community with no stores remaining open, and at about 17 miles left the blacktop and drove on a gravel road that led us against the east wall of the coulee, then into what appeared to be a ranch yard. We passed a few cattle trucks parked beside the road, turned a sharp right curve between a group of buildings, and began climbing a steep hill. We stopped on top of the hill and looked back, thinking we were out of the coulee. But as we drove on, we found that it was simply another branch of the coulee, and it must have created a tremendous waterfall when the meltwater flowed down it.

The road swung over against the right wall, then headed straight toward what appeared to be a blank wall. But when we reached this apparent box canyon, the road made a cut in the canyon face and within a quarter of a mile we were up on the flat plateau again, driving on gravel between fields of ripening wheat. We had left the coulee without being aware of it.

Our route went along straight as a ruler for a short distance, then we came to an intersection, turned left, and went along on a level grade for awhile, then began climbing. When we reached the top of the long hill, we almost immediately started losing altitude again. Soon we were back in Moses Coulee.

Then we found the aerial irrigation we had heard so much about. The system must be a good one because it has been in operation for a long time. The advantage of string-

ing irrigation sprinklers and hoses overhead and anchoring them to each side of the narrow coulee is that they remain in place all the time and don't have to be moved for cultivation or harvesting.

A short distance beyond this example of ingenuity, the Moses Coulee Road joins the major cross-state US Highway 2.

Incidentally, US 2 was at one time the major highway from Seattle to Detroit, and perhaps farther east than that. It is still one of the most scenic highways in the country, closely paralleling the US–Canadian border and following what is now an unbeaten path. It is another alternative to crossing the country on an Interstate.

Ranch midway up Moses Coulee

EASTERN
WASHINGTON

ALL OVER THE NORTHERN PORTION of Washington you can find vivid traces of the Ice Age glaciers: the rubble piled up in the Hood Canal area; Sequim, where glaciers left heaps of gravel; the coulees; the Channeled Scabland; and all through Douglas County, where the glaciers stopped, melted, and dropped their piles of debris.

One side trip through this glacial waste is Washington Highway 172, which turns north off US Highway 2 in the middle of the Big Bend country, where the Columbia River makes a looping turn from east-west to north-south. The turnoff is marked as Farmer on maps, but all that remains of Farmer (if indeed there was ever much more) is a two-story, white, false-fronted building that could have been a store, a schoolhouse, or a Grange hall.

The two-lane blacktop road goes due north for awhile and passes a small village called Withrow, where dozens of locust and evergreen trees have been planted by residents, creating something of an oasis in the wheat fields.

Along the route, especially after the high-

One-building town
of Farmer

way makes a right-angle turn to the east, you will pass piles of boulders left at random on the rolling plain, most of which are basalt picked up by the glaciers north of the Columbia and hauled south a few miles. There is one stretch of 172 just beyond Mansfield where the road suddenly goes through a series of humps and low hills, then straightens out and levels off again. This was one of the biggest glacial dumps in the area.

We stopped in Mansfield for a snack and gasoline, but since it was just before harvest the owner of the town's only café had decided to go on vacation, and a sign in the window informed us we could eat there just over a month from the day we stood at the window. We halted at a service station that had sold us gasoline a few years earlier, but the shelves were bare and the pumps dusty. A friendly woman was inside the building, and she informed us that the only place in town to buy gas was up at the Grange plant just across the railroad.

Our original plan was to get off the beaten track completely and drive back to Highway 2 by way of Jameson Lake, down in Moses Coulee to the south of Mansfield. While the attendant at the Grange plant was making change, we looked at a state map and saw that the road went on through Moses Coulee from Jameson Lake to connect with Highway 2. But experience made me ask if the map was accurate, and the attendant said it was not; that the road still dead-ends at the lake from both directions. I never took the trouble to reckon the precise distance between those two dead ends, but I'll wager it can't be more than two or three miles.

Whatever the cause for this engineering oversight, we were stymied. But it really made little difference. Highway 172 was virtually deserted and my son said I drove like local farmers tend to do; I was rubbernecking and wandered all over the highway, using the center line as a guide for the center of the hood. It makes my son very nervous.

Glacial debris near Mansfield

43

*Winter wheat
being uncovered
by melting snow*

REARDAN TO SPRAGUE

TIME AFTER TIME you'll hear people say they drove across Eastern Washington and didn't see a thing except more of nothing. This is particularly true of people who live in Western Washington and think the only things worth seeing are trees, mountains, and salt water. Poor souls.

True, much of Eastern Washington is flat, and in the summer the subtle scenery is bent and distorted out of shape by heat waves radiating upward from the pavement. But there is as much to see there as in Western Washington if you know what to look for.

This trip over a little-used road is a good example. If July and August aren't your favorite travel months in the near desert of the wheat country, make the trip in the spring while the wheat is still green and growing, or in the autumn when the crop is harvested

and the wheat for next year is just coming out of the ground like rows of tender grass.

If you're driving south from Reardan on Washington Highway 231, you will go across the same kind of landscape you have already been on—rolling hills covered with wheat. You'll go through the picturesque town of Edwall, then climb up a series of low hills with Edwall back to the north.

A short distance further, you'll hit the western edge of the Channeled Scabland, which distinguishes Sprague from the rest of the wheat country. From here on east several miles, the landscape is a miniature canyon country with more barren and walled landscape than you've seen elsewhere in the area.

Without getting into a long discussion of the academic battle that was fought for several decades over the Channeled Scabland,

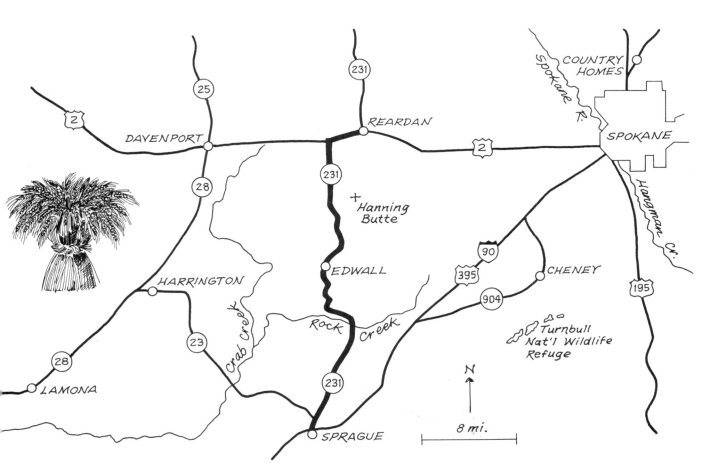

here's a brief explanation of this phenomenon: The discussion over the origin of the Channeled Scabland pitted the traditional geological theories against a new one called catastrophic. The former theories held that all geological formations were the result of eons of natural erosion and other forces. However, after enough geologists accepted the flood theory propounded by a University of Chicago professor named J. Harlan Bretz, they wired him and told him they were all catastrophists.

During one of the Ice Ages, perhaps two or three although nobody is certain how many times it occurred, a great earthen and ice dam was formed over in Montana near Missoula. A vast valley was dammed by this ice and mud, and the lake behind it grew as the glaciers melted. At last the dam gave way, creating one of the worst floods in the history of the world.

The water poured northwestward, scouring out what became the group of lakes in Northern Idaho. It swept across to the site of Spokane, then gradually swung south and went the length of the state to the Washington–Oregon border where it joined the Columbia River and was contained within the Columbia River Gorge.

As the water traveled south—an epic flash flood—it scoured off all the soil that had accumulated over the centuries, exposing the basalt beneath and leaving the canyons, buttes, and jumbled loose rocks. Its course was roughly 30 miles wide and varied according to local topography. Its force was dissipated somewhat the farther south it went.

In the Sprague area you can see ample evidence of the flood's passing: the finger lakes in the area pointing generally northeast, the barren and broken basalt landscape, and on the eastern edge the sudden reappearance of good Palouse soil that is up to 100 feet deep in places. For a complete tour across this kind of landscape, follow Washington Highway 23 southeast out of Sprague to US Highway 195 in Steptoe.

Facing page:
*Wheat stubble
and newly seeded
land near Edwall*

Below:
*Crab Creek Valley
and Saddle Mountains*

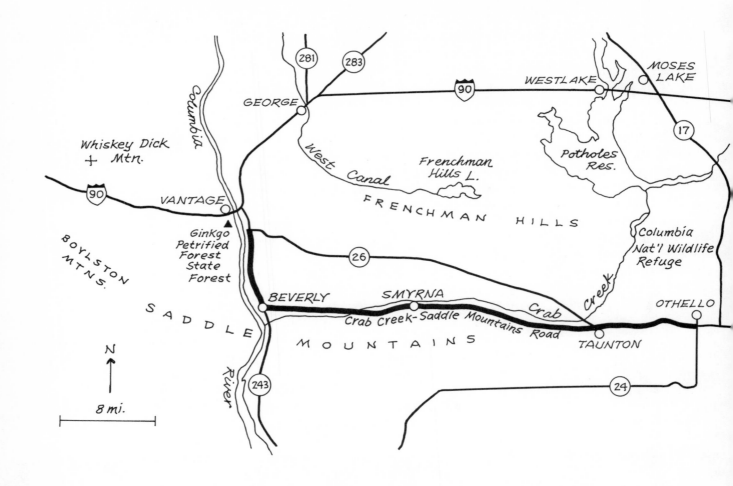

CRAB CREEK VALLEY

CRAB CREEK is one of the longest small streams in the state. It begins near Spokane and wanders west across the barren wheat country to Soap Lake. Then it swings south into Moses Lake and the Potholes Reservoir, emerges, and goes south almost to Othello. Then it wanders due east along the base of the Saddle Mountains and enters the Columbia River at Beverly.

The last few miles of the creek's route are through one of the prettiest areas in the Columbia Basin irrigation project. Crab Creek by this time is so laden with nutrients from the irrigated land that the fishing along the base of the Saddle Mountains is famous throughout the Northwest. In this broad val-

ley bordered on the north by Frenchman Hills are several small lakes, called seep lakes because underground water from the irrigated fields follows the line of impervious hardpan underground until it surfaces at a lower elevation. So in the Crab Creek Valley the small lakes are rich with food for trout, and they grow quickly to sizes not ordinarily found in lakes so heavily fished.

You don't have to be a fisherman to enjoy the valley. If you like desert scenery, this is an excellent drive.

Start at the tiny town of Beverly, which was built when the electric Milwaukee Road stretched its tracks down the valley and across the Columbia River here. The Crab

48

Creek–Saddle Mountains Road constitutes Beverly's main street, and as soon as you top a slight rise in town, the barren buttes of the mountains show on the south side of the creek. The road is paved a short distance and is gravel the rest of the way to the main highway where you connect near Othello.

There are acres of sand dunes along the base of the mountains, piled up there by winds down the Columbia River, and some have been set aside for offroad vehicles.

You will cross Crab Creek occasionally on low bridges that give you nice views across the marsh and cattails, and you will go past the sidings of Smyrna and Taunton. Overhead, the mountain scenery changes from mile to mile. One stretch is deeply and wildly carved by the weather into spires, castles, and other shapes. Sometimes an outcropping of various colors will show.

You may be taken almost by surprise when the road makes a cut in the low basaltic formation and unexpectedly climbs up out of the valley where the mountains peter out into rolling hills. Then the road turns sharply to the north and joins Washington Highway 26 just outside Othello.

My son and I visited the valley to take photographs for this book, and emerged at Beverly late in the afternoon, then drove back up the Columbia to rejoin Interstate 90 and head for home. But before we were on the Interstate, we were treated to one of those little adventures that you learn to take for granted while traveling the little-used highways.

We were at the intersection of Washington Highways 243 and 26 waiting for trucks to pass when a semi loaded with baled hay came down the steep grade into the Columbia River Valley and turned the sharp curve directly ahead of us. A whole section of the bales flew off and scattered all over the highway and into the ditch.

We parked and ran back to help clear the hay off the highway before a car hit it. Another car also pulled over, and another truck loaded with hay. The first truck driver said

he had told the other trucker on his CB radio that he had dropped his load.

Only then did I see a man sitting on one of the bales beside the road. I ran over and asked him if he was all right, because he certainly didn't look all right at all. He was covered with hay, chaff, and dust, and sat on the bale with his head in his hands.

"I think so," he said. "I'll be all right in a minute."

He didn't have a tooth in his head, and he hadn't shaved in a day or two.

"I was just walking along when he dumped his load on me," he said, getting a little more strength in his voice. "Knocked my feet right out from under me. My cigarette lighter is laying way over there," he continued, pointing toward the deep ditch. The truck driver and I stopped working to listen.

He kept talking, saying he would like to get that truck driver's name, and that he would have a few things to say to him when they met.

"I was just walking along when, boom!, he got me," he told us. "I ran out of gas up at Moses Lake and was walking down here where I've got a cache of gas behind some rocks up the hill."

Moses Lake is at least 40 miles away, and neither I nor the truck driver believed he had walked that far in the hot sun to pick up a can of gasoline he had cached in a pile of rocks.

"I'll give you good odds he was hiding in that load of hay when the load parted and fell off with him in it," the driver said. "I don't know about you, but I don't believe a word he has said."

I didn't know, and still don't. The longer the victim talked, the more he elaborated on his story, and I suspect the truck driver was right. Either way—having a load of hay dumped on you while you were walking along a highway, or stealing a ride in a load of hay when it falls off the truck and takes you with it—it would make you think the gods of circumstance were feeling particularly mean that day.

49

WASHTUCNA, BENGE, AND RALSTON

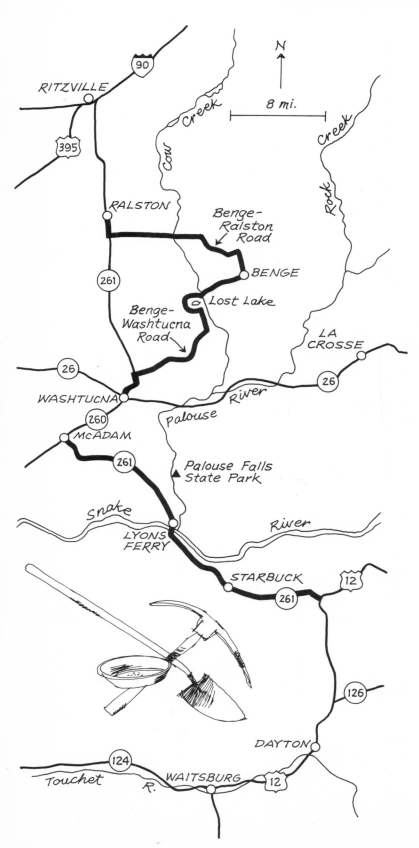

ONE WINTER MORNING I was returning from Washtucna to Seattle in the second car I owned, an old Chevrolet coupe with woefully inadequate defrosters. I stopped and stepped out of the car to scrape off the ice, and took a classic pratfall. I quickly got back to my feet and looked around to see who had witnessed the event. There was nobody in sight, not even a farmhouse. Feeling better about things, I tested the road and found that I had been driving on the invisible "black ice" for several miles. The rest of my trip to the summit of Snoqualmie Pass was much slower.

I have made the trip dozens of times, and have frequently taken side trips off the main routes on the spur of the moment. Very few roads dead-end in the wheat country, and all but the newest reasonably follow the township lines from point to point instead of arrogantly cutting across the good farmland.

One pleasant drive that gives you a bit of relief from the open, flat scenery (if that bothers you; it doesn't me) is a loop from Washtucna to Benge and back to the highway at Ralston.

Go north of Washtucna about two miles on Washington Highway 261 toward Ritzville, and turn east on the Benge–Washtucna Road. It follows a depression called a draw with wheat fields on the steep hillsides on both sides of the road and an occasional cattle ranch along the way. Soon the road joins the Burlington Northern tracks along a broad valley with Cow Creek running through it toward the Palouse River.

Just after railroad, road, and creek converge, there is a dirt road leading off to the west past Lost Lake, which a friend and I learned is a good name for it. We drove the road one day and couldn't find any trace of the lake.

The Old Mullan Road, the local name for the Mullan Military Road built between Fort Walla Walla and Fort Benton, Montana, in 1858, follows this valley a short distance

Facing page:
Palouse Falls during heavy spring runoff

before striking off due north across the barren and rolling land. Traces of the wagon tracks occasionally can be seen along ledges above the valley, and nearly every fall a number of local horsemen get together to follow sections of the trail.

Benge is a very small town with only a scattering of buildings and a single store that was open on our last trip through. As farms grow larger and larger, some small towns' population dwindles, and more and more farmers move to a central town and drive to the farm each day. Consequently, the smallest towns get smaller while the larger ones seem to stay fairly constant in population.

From Benge, take the Ralston–Benge Road, which turns north out of town and then turns sharply to the west just above town. It crosses the Mullan route again, then crosses Cow Creek in a picturesque, shallow canyon with ship-shaped rocks and buttes nearby. Nearly all such formations point in a north-by-northeast direction and were carved by the catastrophic floods following the last Ice Age.

From this Cow Creek crossing, the road heads straight west with only one or two jogs and connects with Highway 261 about three miles south of Ralston. If railroad towns like Ralston have a familiar ring, it is because they were named by the railroad companies. In this case, the town was named for what is now Ralston–Purina Company, one of the railroad's prime accounts at that time.

Facing page:
Crab Creek Valley

Below:
Field near Benge

*Old farm
equipment near
Washtucna*

*Palouse Falls,
only a trickle
by late summer*

PALOUSE FALLS AND SNAKE RIVER CANYON

DESPITE THE NATIONAL ORGY of bull-dozing and earth moving we suffered between the close of World War II and the present, there are still a few places that don't have many roads. The Palouse River Canyon and the Snake River are two examples. The few glimpses we do get of them show us some very rugged country, as rugged as the more famous Hells Canyon on the Snake River between Idaho and Oregon. Since it isn't as deep, it isn't as famous.

The Snake River portion of the Lewis and Clark Expedition of 1804–06 was one of the toughest water routes the explorers experienced, and until dam-building expertise improved, the Snake River was a bane to steamboaters and towboat skippers. A lot of rocks are named for these men, usually to commemorate the wreck of a steamboat or grain barge. One towboat skipper had a system for beginning a turn on the Snake. When he could see a particular tree through the doors of a barn on the bank, he began his turn. Unfortunately, the story goes, the doors were closed one day and he stacked up his barges on the bank.

The Palouse River Canyon runs mostly through private property and can be seen only along Washington Highway 26 between Washtucna and Lacrosse, but the deepest portion runs south of here just before joining the Snake River at Lyons Ferry. There is a farmer's road into the Little Falls of the Palouse, but the property is posted against trespassing. You will have to be content to see the canyon at Palouse Falls State Park, between McAdam and Lyons Ferry, on Washington Highway 261, and at the state park at Lyons Ferry.

As an aside, the Palouse River was named Drewyer's River by Lewis and Clark in honor of their most valuable expedition member. However, late arrivals named it for the local Indians and so the invaluable Drouillard (Drewyer) has left his name on no map.

A good way to see these canyons is to follow the dirt road of Highway 261 from the grain elevator named McAdam down to Palouse Falls State Park. The road goes over hilly ground with an occasional scoured-out canyon along the way, part of the damage done by the so-called Spokane Flood, which created the Channeled Scabland. From the park you can see Palouse Falls, of course, which may be only a trickle if you visit in late summer, or a deluge in the spring and winter. You can see almost to the end of the canyon from the park, but your line of sight ends where the gorge bends to the right before entering the Snake River.

Just upstream from the state park at Lyons Ferry is the Marmes Rockshelter, where the oldest human skeletal remains in America at that time were found in 1965. Washington State University archaeologists worked in the shallow cave for several months but were evicted by the backwaters of Ice Harbor Dam just downstream on the Snake.

As evidence that everything isn't wasted in America, the high, narrow bridge that crosses the Snake River at Lyons Ferry was salvaged from the Columbia River crossing at Vantage and reconstructed at its present site.

The highway follows the south side of the Snake a few miles, giving some good views of the nearly submerged canyon with a few islands protruding. Then the road turns south away from the river into Starbuck and onward to connect with the major highway between Walla Walla and Clarkston, US Highway 12.

An alternative route if you're going to the Tri-Cities of Richland, Pasco, and Kennewick, is to take the dirt road immediately south of the Lyons Ferry bridge that will take you past the small communities of Clyde, Walker, and Eureka before joining Washington Highway 124.

57

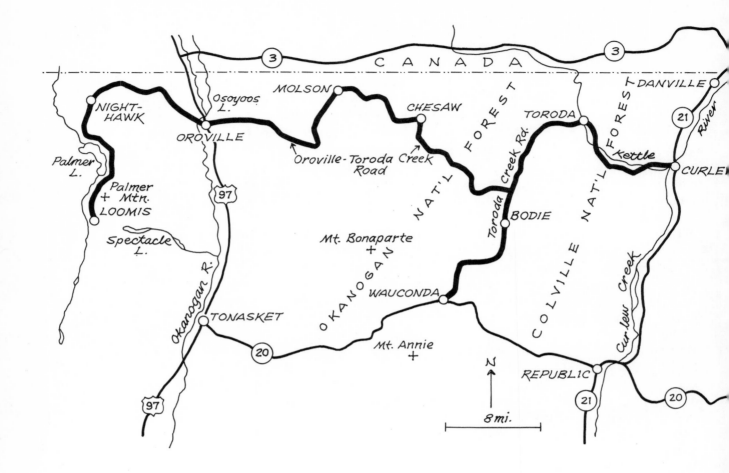

OROVILLE AND MOLSON

TO ME, the Okanogan Country of north-central Washington is a very special part of the state. I use the term Okanogan Country as loosely as other city slickers in the state to encompass nearly everything from the Nighthawk–Loomis area east to the Idaho border. But the more accurate geographical breakdown of this series of ranges and ridges that run generally north-south all the way across the top of the state and down to the Columbia River would include the Okanogan Highlands, the Kettle River Range, the Selkirk Range, and the Pend Oreille area.

As I drove one stretch of highway, unbothered by other traffic, I knew I was going to impose my enthusiasm on readers and hoped they wouldn't mind. So this is a warning: You're going to be exposed to wide open

spaces, tall timber, abandoned farmhouses, rushing rivers, and one babbling author.

A good way to start your backroad exploring is to drive north on US/Washington Highway 97 to the pretty town of Oroville nearly on the Canadian border. Stop here to top off your gas tank and·take the Oroville–Toroda Creek Road east out of town. You'll quickly leave the town behind as you pass orchards with small houses for pickers. Then you start climbing out of the valley on an oiled road and up to the high plateau, which is mostly barren and broken country. After about eight miles, you'll see a road heading north toward Molson and the Canadian border. This road goes through ranches, and you'll occasionally pass piles of rocks collected by the farmers and outcroppings left

Restored buildings of Molson

behind by the glaciers that once covered this area.

You turn a curve and suddenly you're in the nearly ghost town of Molson. Much of it is now a museum. Half a dozen buildings have been preserved and are jammed full of antiques and historic farm machinery. Inside the general store is a collection of photographs telling the strange history of this town (or towns to be more accurate).

Gold, in the Poland China Mine up near the Canadian border, created the need for the first town. The area around the mine wasn't suitable for a town, so John Molson, who had money, and George Meacham, a promoter, formed a partnership and laid out a town in 1900 and named it Molson. Within a year it had a population of 300 on an investment by Molson of some $75,000. The new town had a drugstore, a dentist, and a lawyer in addition to the general store. A newspaper

was set up, although nobody is quite certain if it ever printed an issue.

The hotel, named Tonasket Hotel, was quite elaborate, boasting three stories, a number of large windows, and a wrap-around ballustrade.

Then, with all this accomplished, the Poland China Mine began petering out and the population dropped. Next, homesteaders began arriving. A grain warehouse and a new store were built in 1904, and a year later a rumor was spread that a railroad was coming through, and it did. Saloons opened and a deputy was hired to keep the peace. Lots were selling at a premium, but they had a fatal flaw that appeared when a man named J. H. McDonald filed a homestead. Forty acres of his 160-acre homestead included nearly all of Molson, Hotel Tonasket and all. Nobody else had bothered to claim the land by legal means.

59

The lawyer and his colleagues elsewhere harvested a crop of lawsuits. Gunfights were threatened over trespassing. In order to keep the town alive, another one was laid out after McDonald built a fence around his share of what became known as Old Molson. A bank had been constructed there, and it was put on skids and dragged to New Molson just down the road a piece. The bank still didn't have a permanent home, and for several days it opened for business at a different location every morning. Finally, amid some ceremony and relief, it was assigned a permanent location. The grand opening was spoiled only by a street fight that erupted when too many Molsonites got together in one place.

Finally the two towns found one thing they could agree on: They built a three-story brick school almost exactly midway between Old and New Molson, sharing the cost in the noble belief that their children should receive a good education, and that neither town could afford an adequate school alone. This created still another town, Center Molson, which became something of a demilitarized zone between the two towns. If one town got a theater, the other had to have one, and this civic pride and/or jealousy brought carbon copies of auto dealerships and other businesses.

The Post Office Department would allot only one post office to the three towns, and Old Molson had it. So New Molson fought to get one of its citizens appointed postmaster. They were successful in 1920, but they couldn't get the post office moved to New Molson, and the Old Molson postmaster wouldn't leave his post. So one day while he was at lunch, New Molson patriots simply stole the post office.

Eventually both towns had to give up the struggle because the whole area was becoming depopulated. Mining was no longer a major economic factor, and the railroad tracks were unceremoniously torn up and hauled away. The school stands vacant today, as do most of the remaining buildings. The fight over three towns is of academic and museum interest only.

The gravel road toward Chesaw goes up a hill behind Molson, giving a good view of the remnants of the three towns, then takes you through more open but broken landscape and past a number of abandoned farmhouses and barns that have turned a rich brown over the years. The road had been recently graded before I traveled over it, but this seemed to have broken loose more rocks than it removed. So it was with considerable relief that I reached the intersection where a paved road appeared, which is the continuation of the Oroville–Toroda Creek Road.

Chesaw, named for a Chinese innkeeper married to an Indian, used to be a ghost town of sorts, but no longer. There were perhaps half a dozen cars parked outside the grocery, and several buildings along the main street had been restored, spruced up, and in some cases even painted. I can't explain why, but I resent ghost towns being revived. It probably doesn't apply to Chesaw —I didn't even stop when I saw the improvements—but too often ghost towns become Virginia Cities and Tombstones and the like. If not that, they become artsy-cutesy, which makes me even grouchier and impatient to be somewhere else.

The drive from Chesaw to Toroda Creek Road is one of the most delightful in this part of the state. It wanders in and out of the Okanogan National Forest and is paved most of the way. Most of it is along the north fork of Beaver Creek, and there are several small lakes beside the highway, some with camping areas, others simply still water covered with a bright green algae.

This road intersects with the Toroda Creek Road just north of the ghost town of Bodie. You have your choice here of turning south toward Bodie and Wauconda and back to the Okanogan River Valley at Tonasket, or going north toward Curlew or west toward Republic.

*Farming and mining
equipment in outdoor
Molson museum*

61

CURLEW TO WAUCONDA

THIS TRIP offers more of the same type of scenery glowingly described in the previous section. This whole chunk of low mountains in a dry climate more closely resembles the Rocky Mountains than the damp Cascade Range. The mountains tend to be granite and the timber is quaking aspen, pine, and tamarack, with a minimum of underbrush.

From the tiny town of Curlew, the highway follows the Kettle River faithfully around several wide bends, through the pleasant forest, and beneath sheer bluffs. In late summer the riverbed is exposed, with wide gravel bars bleached white in the sun in contrast to the swift, clear water.

At the site of Toroda, only one or two buildings, the road turns southwest—otherwise you'll hit the Canadian border at Midway—and follows Toroda Creek nearly the whole way to Wauconda on Washington Highway 20. But before that happens, you will pass right through the middle of the ghost town of Bodie, a former milling town. On the right or north side of the road is the old schoolhouse with twin outhouses out back. Across the road behind a fence are four or five other smaller buildings that were stores and blacksmith shops and so forth. The buildings haven't been ravaged by souvenir hunters, pyromaniacs, or interior decorators who use the weathered wood for office and home interiors.

The road continues on southwest, past ranches and along the edges of hillsides until it emerges at Wauconda, a town with little more than a post office, café, store, and service station. But it enjoys a grand view down a valley to the south.

Facing page:
*Ranch near
Wauconda*

Below: *All that
remains of Bodie
homes*

*Similkameen Canyon
and reservoir*

NIGHTHAWK AND LOOMIS

THIS SHORT LOOP from Oroville back toward the Cascade Mountains is one of the nicest trips you'll find in the Okanogan Highlands, and one of the most historic so far as the state's literature is concerned.

The road leaves the center of Oroville and heads west up into the beautiful Similkameen Gorge with the river flowing down below the highway from Palmer Lake. The road takes a sharp turn to the south just above Nighthawk with the main highway here going on north into Canada.

Somebody told me Nighthawk was a ghost town, and I drove there expecting little or no population. Nothing could be farther from the truth. There are a couple of the old buildings remaining, almost hanging out over the Similkameen River, but they are surrounded by modern homes and orchards. Orchards appear to have taken over the whole valley all the way from Nighthawk down through Loomis and along the route

back to the Okanogan Valley just above Tonasket. The valley is literally covered with fruit trees and berry vines.

Just below Nighthawk the road swings around the east bank of Palmer Lake with Mount Ellemeham and Palmer Mountain looming up over it, creating one of the picture-postcard scenes you hope for when visiting a lake. The road along the lake is narrow and gives the impression that the orchards and vines could crowd it off into the water at any moment.

Another few miles and you are in Loomis, made famous by an Easterner who didn't like life as an architect after graduating from Harvard. Guy Waring dropped out, so to speak, and moved his family to the West. They came to Portland, Oregon, first, and he worked on a railroad to support his wife and three children. He heard of the Okanogan Country and moved to the Loomis–Oroville area and was a cowboy, storekeeper, barber, cook, farmer, shoemaker, fur trader, carpenter, and justice of the peace. He even tried his hand at taking in laundry to earn a living.

He had been a friend of Theodore Roosevelt and Owen Wister while in college, and was one of the reasons Wister came to Washington, the Winthrop area in his case, before he wrote his classic Western novel, *The Virginian*.

During his later years, Waring wrote an autobiographical account of his years in the Okanogan and meant it for distribution among his friends and family. But the book became a modest seller and is accepted as one of the best written on the Pacific Northwest. From the opening words—"As I recall the ranch flooded with the yellow sunlight my heart is stirred as by no other memory" —through such keen observations as this one about a hotel in Coulee City—"At Coulee City the branch train arrived too late for the stage which took you to Bridgeport on the Columbia River. Train and stage were scheduled to miss each other, and were invariably faithful to schedule. Had they connected the hotel would have died . . ."— Waring gave us a view of the state's pioneer years that few other books have seriously attempted.

A public campground has been established on the southern end of Palmer Lake, and it is a very special place late in the day when the sun begins dropping behind the mountains and dark shadows start to spread over the surface of the lake.

*Evening shadows
south of Nighthawk*

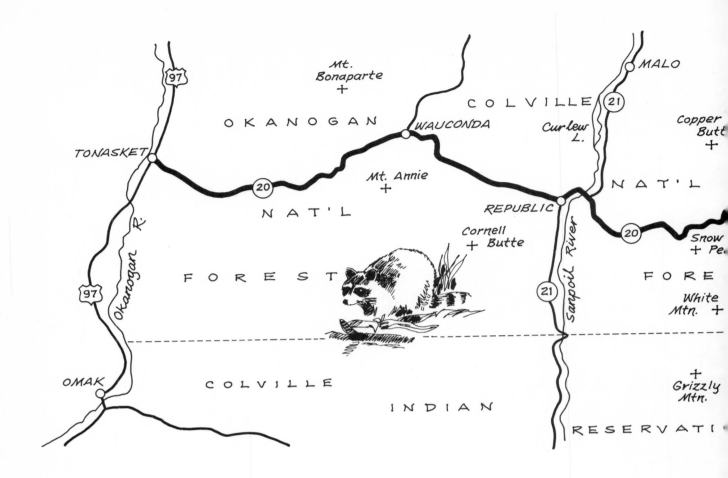

TIGER TO TONASKET

RESIDENTS OF THE AREA might object to my calling the major highway across Northern Washington a backroad, but no offense is intended. The drive is so beautiful, and the trip usually such a quiet one, that Washington Highway 20 qualifies as a backroad. After you travel it, you'll have to agree it bears absolutely no resemblance to an Interstate highway, and little resemblance to the major cross-state highways farther south.

The whole highway runs through some of the state's most scenic areas. It begins near Port Townsend, jumps across Puget Sound to Whidbey Island, and then becomes the North Cascades Highway, emerging from the Cascades at Okanogan. Here it joins US Highway 97 to Tonasket, then swings east again and runs almost to the Idaho border at Tiger before heading south along the Pend Oreille River to Newport. The route between

Tiger and Tonasket is one of the least-traveled portions of Washington 20 and the most scenic part east of the Cascades.

If you take the Pend Oreille River trip and cross west to Ione, you will drive south a short distance to Tiger and turn west. Tiger isn't a town any longer, but it deserves to remain on maps because the listing empty store—post office at the junction is beautifully run down.

From here, Highway 20 begins climbing out of the valley and up into the timber, twisting and turning and occasionally giving you wide-angle views of the valley you've just left behind. When the highway levels off on top, you are in lake, pine, and pasture country. There are a number of lakes along the highway, or just off it a few hundred yards, which make excellent picnic stops. After descending the low range and follow-

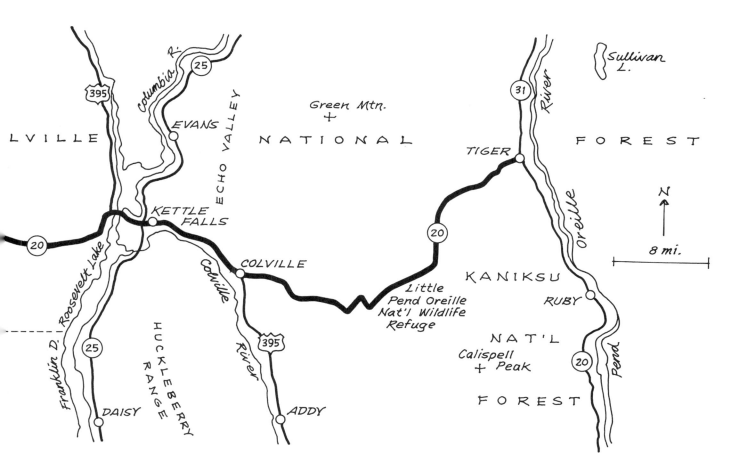

ing the Little Pend Oreille River into Colville, the largest town in the area, the route continues on west to the smaller town of Kettle Falls beside the Columbia River's Roosevelt Lake, the backwaters of Grand Coulee Dam far to the south.

The highway climbs again into the Kettle River Range and finally reaches the summit at Sherman Pass, the state's highest mountain pass at 5,575 feet. There is a scenic viewpoint at the summit that presents the range undulating off in several directions.

From here down to Republic the highway runs through avenues of tall trees, along narrow shelves above the canyon below, and finally joins O'Brien Creek for the last few miles into Republic.

Republic is gold-mining country, with streets named for the big discoveries around North America, including Klondike and a few other similar names. Its gold rush occurred at almost the exact time the major discovery was made on the Klondike River in

the Yukon, 1896, and gold is still being mined in the area. During the mining heyday around the turn of the century, the people of Republic were like all other boomtowners in hoping their town would become a major metropolis. There was so much talk about a railroad coming into town that it was dubbed "The Hot Air Line" since that was all many expected to come of it. But a line was built from Republic to Grand Forks, British Columbia, in 1902, and later that year was taken over by the Great Northern.

From Republic the highway winds pleasantly down a valley toward Tonasket and intersects with the Chesaw–Curlew Road at Wauconda. About halfway between Wauconda and Tonasket is another intersection with the Aeneas Valley Road, which meanders down the broad valley into the Colville Indian Reservation and joins Washington Highway 21 between Republic and the Columbia River just upstream from Grand Coulee Dam.

*Crystal Falls
on Washington 20*

Palouse River Canyon

Mount Rainier

*View from
Sherman Pass,
looking east*

*Kettle River
near Curlew*

PEND OREILLE RIVER

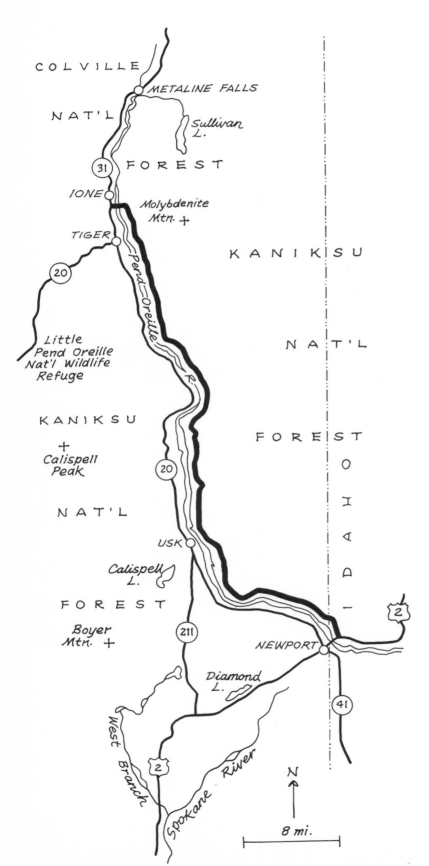

COLVILLE
NAT'L
FOREST

METALINE FALLS

Sullivan L.

31

IONE

Molybdenite Mtn. +

TIGER

20

Little
Pend Oreille
Nat'l Wildlife
Refuge

KANIKSU

+ Calispell Peak

NAT'L

USK

Calispell L.

FOREST

Boyer Mtn. +

211

Pend—Oreille R.

KANIKSU

NAT'L

FOREST

IDAHO

2

NEWPORT

41

Diamond L.

West Branch

Spokane River

2

N

8 mi.

IT DOESN'T MAKE MUCH DIFFERENCE which side of the Pend Oreille River you choose for a drive north out of Newport. Although Washington Highway 20 on the west side is more heavily traveled than the real backroad on the east side, either will give you excellent scenery without heavy traffic. I would recommend the east side because when I traveled it in the middle of summer there was so little traffic that I could stop in the center of the paved road to gawk without fear of creating a major traffic event.

Whichever side you choose, you will be driving in a valley surrounded by the Selkirk Range, a spur of the Rockies that cuts through Northern Idaho and into Northeastern Washington and British Columbia. The mountains are well worn along here, both by the natural forces of erosion and the Ice Age glaciers that created the valleys and took the edges and peaks off the granite mountains. Occasionally you will see dark basalt outcroppings, but for the most part these are very old mountains that surround the flat valleys between.

The road begins in Idaho but quickly crosses the Pend Oreille River bridge into Washington. The Pend Oreille River is flat and usually calm along here, giving you excellent reflections of the trees, sky, and clouds. But before you start the trip, it is a good idea to prowl around Newport a bit. Originally Newport was a village across the river in Idaho, and its first residents had to get provisions from Sand Point, a town several miles away on Lake Pend Oreille, either by trail or by boat on the river. A steamboat was put into service on the river in the 1890s and a town called New Port was founded on the Washington side of the river. The original village, also New Port, was called Old Town. After the Great Northern railway appeared in New Port, the Idaho residents moved across the river, or as the official report says: "Newport, Idaho, moved 3,175 feet to Newport, Washington."

The riverfront portion of Newport is still called Old Town, and you will go through it on the way across the bridge to the start of this road.

The route follows the river most of the way, and various state and federal agencies have built a string of campgrounds along the bank. The Kalispel Indian Reservation takes up one long, narrow strip of the riverbank and you'll know when you are in it by the highway signs, an arrowhead with the numeral 5 inside it. You can cross the river to Highway 20 at Usk, or drive several miles north and cross at the mill town of Ione.

Reflections on
Pend Oreille River

The Cascade Range

COMPARED WITH THE ROCKY MOUNTAINS or even the Sierra Nevada, the Cascade Range isn't that impressive. It is a low range with only its volcanoes—Mount Rainier, Mount Adams, Mount St. Helens, and Mount Baker—protruding above the 10,000-foot level. Only one of the major passes—Washington Pass in the North Cascades—is more than 5,000 feet above sea level, and the highest pass in the state is Sherman Pass (5,575 feet) in the Okanogan Highlands. So travelers in Washington don't have to worry about altitude sickness or nosebleeds while traveling in the Cascades.

This range starts in Canada and eventually meets the Sierra Nevada in California with only one interruption in its course—the Columbia River, which has cut a gash through it. Otherwise, the Cascades separate Washington into two distinct climatological zones. To people on its western side, the range serves as a barrier against the frigid arctic air and storms of winter. While blizzards blow in Eastern Washington and the temperature stays below freezing for days or weeks, the western slopes will be a balmy 40 or 50 degrees. This barrier also keeps most of the damp marine air from the Pacific on the western side of the mountains, making that part of the state much more humid and frequently

Facing page: Clouds drifting through timber in northern Cascades

Sun in second-growth timber in the Central Cascades

overcast. It also makes the western slopes some of the best Douglas fir country in the world, and logging was a major factor in the state's early economy, as it still is.

As much as environmentalists complain about logging, most of the Cascades would be inaccessible today were it not for that industry. Logging roads have become thoroughfares, and, particularly in Gifford Pinchot National Forest, those logging roads have become excellent paved highways that permit us backroaders to drive nearly anywhere in the mountains on a weekend, or even on a day trip. This isn't an effort to condone all logging practices. Few things are more distressing to a scenery lover than seeing one of the major peaks off in the distance with piles of logging debris, most of which could be utilized instead of wasted, littered all over the landscape between you and the peak. Even a burned-over forest area is more picturesque than a logged-over landscape; at least it is a natural scene. Enough such talk; this can lead to ranting.

Compared with most major ranges in North America, the Cascades are young, something like 50 million years old, give or take 5 or 10 million. They gradually uplifted from the ocean floor and created a great saltwater inland sea that had the Rocky Mountains as its eastern shore. Gradually the sea evaporated, leaving behind fossils of marine creatures all across the Great American Desert.

It is interesting to note while driving across the state how quickly the climate changes. All the way from the coast to the summit of the range, you are in a damp climate with timber so thick you sometimes feel you're driving in an evergreen tunnel. But once you reach the crest, the timber thins out quickly and in a matter of only a few minutes you leave the western dampness for the dryness of the eastern slopes with sparse timber that has by now become pine and tamarack. Meadows frequently appear and instead of thick underbrush, there is bare ground beneath the trees.

This transition is equally dramatic while driving along the Columbia River Gorge, and in the summer you can see the change in scenery and climate much faster than while crossing one of the passes. In the gorge you will most likely be buffeted about by strong winds that sweep up and down the river unobstructed by the mountains. These same winds that come in from the coast, laden with moisture, are swept up over the mountains, then down the eastern slopes, pressed down by the heavy atmosphere and dried and heated in the process. All across the eastern edge of the range you'll notice trees permanently bent in one direction, away from the mountains, because the wind is frequent, strong, and predictable as a river.

One of the most exciting events a backroader can experience is standing on a high mountain and watching the processes of weather at work. This happened to me while I was on top of Burley Mountain pondering the drive back down again. All the major peaks were visible beneath a high cloud cover and I was grumbling to myself that the sun wasn't breaking through to make my photographs more colorful and cheerful. Then, off to the south below Mount St. Helens, a shower started falling on the wooded slopes, slowly moving east toward Mount Adams. A few drops descended on me, so I put the camera gear back in the car and watched the cloud move across Mount Adams, distorting its image as though I were looking at it through inferior glass. Then the rain and the cloud from which it came disappeared as it hit the warm and dry air of the eastern side of the mountains.

It wasn't much of an event by mountaineering standards. After all, I had escaped no avalanches, and no bolts of lightning struck near me. But it was one of those small events that cannot be captured on film yet linger long in the memory.

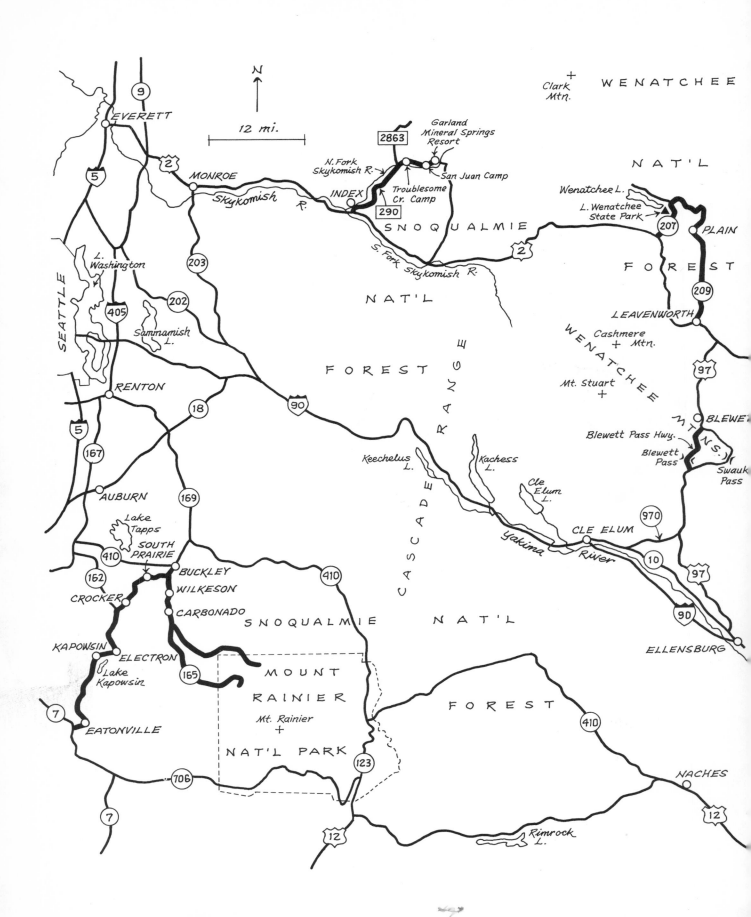

*North Fork of the
Skykomish River
near Garland Mineral
Springs*

GARLAND MINERAL SPRINGS

IT WAS very early in the morning when we drove up US Highway 2 and turned north on Road 290 toward the small town of Index, a picturesque little village huddled beneath the towering peaks of the North Cascades. The logging trucks weren't out yet and we had the road entirely to ourselves. The road faithfully follows the North Fork of the Skykomish River up the canyon floor, past mailboxes of homes hidden back in the dense timber, over numerous small streams, and down avenues of Douglas fir through which the sun only occasionally penetrates.

The road is paved 15 miles into the mountains and comes equipped with enough flat turnouts to let you stop, walk back, and take a photo of that pretty creek or clump of giant devil's club. As the road begins to climb into thinning timber, the river can be seen more

often. The farther you go the more likely you are to see small cabins and mobile homes back in the timber, stove pipes puffing gray smoke in the morning chill.

As we drove we wondered how it is that some roads, such as this one, are chosen to be paved while others with more residents and more attractions remain gravel or dirt. Assuming it had something to do with politics—we blame all things beyond our understanding on politics—we continued on toward the end of the blacktop, and saw our first logging truck at the intersection of Road No. 2863, which comes down from the high country past two or three abandoned mines and the vanished town of Galena.

The Forest Service has two campgrounds just beyond this intersection, Troublesome Creek and San Juan. Both have been there for

81

*Trout Creek
emptying into the
North Fork of the
Skykomish River*

decades and both are popular destinations for car and RV campers because of the beautiful waterfalls nearby, and the pavement keeps the dust down. However, on this July morning there were fewer than half a dozen camping parties in the campgrounds.

The pavement ends about a mile beyond San Juan Campground, and off to the right near the river is a cluster of wooden buildings that used to be Garland Mineral Springs Resort. The mineral springs emit a rather unpleasant lukewarm water with a salty taste. But the area is closed to the public now, so we drove on up the gravel road a short distance and over a bridge that gave us a great view of the North Fork of the Skykomish River curving against a bluff and Bear Mountain in the background.

We planned to continue on a few miles,

and perhaps even follow the rough road back around and come out on Highway 2 again in Skykomish, our breakfast stop. Just as we started up a long hill, though, we saw a sign warning us that logging operations were under way on the road. We have found loggers to be reasonable people with whom to share the backroads, and log-truck drivers invariably polite. But driving a car not much larger than a pampered dog's kennel, we wondered if we would even be seen beside those trucks and other giant equipment. So with few regrets, we turned around in the middle of the road and headed back toward Index. On the very first curve we came face to face with a logging truck. It wasn't an eyeball-to-eyeball confrontation at all; more of an eyeball-to-hubcap situation. We coexisted on the road momentarily, and I fled.

PLAIN

A BROAD VALLEY with snow-capped mountains around it in the spring, great cross-country skiing in the winter. One of the state's prettiest rivers for kayaking or inflatable rafting. Fields of new-mown hay curing in the sun, and local traffic that moves at the regal speed of 30 miles per hour. The Plain area looks like one of those places progress and haste ignored in their rush to get somewhere else.

Take Washington Highway 207 east off US Highway 2 where it swings almost due south toward the Tumwater Canyon and Leavenworth. Highway 207 goes down a broad avenue of trees toward Lake Wenatchee, where there is a large state park plus one or two primitive campgrounds, and eventually winds around the lake to end on the edge of the high country behind the lake.

But to take the Plain route, turn east on Washington Highway 209 a short distance beyond the state park entrance and follow 209 to its end in Leavenworth. You will go past several farms in the beautiful valley, through the collection of homes and a church constituting Plain (no store, though). At the

The meadows of Plain area

head of the valley you will curve and switch-back up out of the valley to the timbered slopes again, and each switchback has a broad shelf with plenty of room to park and enjoy the view. You cross the Wenatchee River, and this section, from headwaters at Lake Wenatchee to Highway 2, is very popular for river rats. However, it is popular with nobody when it enters Tumwater Canyon above Leavenworth, so be certain you know where to take out before you begin. Otherwise, you will go over a waterfall or two.

Once the road gets back on top, it dips down occasionally into picturesque little valleys and skirts around farms rather than cutting through them. It returns to Highway 2 on the east edge of Leavenworth.

A suggestion: If you have never been along this route, try to make it a loop trip during the autumn when the leaves are turning. All along the Plain route (Highways 207 and 209) and especially in Tumwater Canyon, the autumn colors are fantastic in late September.

Wenatchee River near Plain

BLEWETT PASS

YOU HAVE no doubt perceived by now that I am addicted to unpopulated places. I like people. Honest. I just don't like them cluttering up my scenery. So when I went looking for Blewett Pass, I was certain I could drive down the middle of the road and rubberneck to my heart's content.

But first I had to find the blasted road. On a previous trip on US Highway 97 between Interstate 90 and US Highway 2, going south, I had watched for the turn in a haphazard sort of way so I could catch the old Blewett Pass route on a future trip. If there was a sign marking the old pass, I didn't see it. Assuming the sign was there and I had missed it, I gave it no more thought until I struck out looking for it seriously.

For the first time since I've lived in Washington, I did make it a point to stop at the old mining arrastra, an ore-grinder made of a single stone, at what little is left of the ghost mining town of Blewett. Arrastras were only a slight improvement over pestles Indians and druggists use.

Judging from my Forest Service map, the Blewett Pass turnoff wasn't far south of there, so I pulled over almost onto the shoulder and drove like a Sunday driver for just over a mile when I saw some ramshackle cabins off to the west and a road that leads past them. Taking a chance, I turned off on the road and immediately found myself on a one-lane bridge with a raised roadway made of planks, staring at a sign stating this was,

Switchback on Blewett Pass Highway

THE CASCADE RANGE

indeed, the Blewett Pass Highway and was being protected as a one-lane road after a fashion by the Forest Service. Eureka! I felt like Daniel Boone in the wilderness, a real pathfinder.

The road is narrow all the way up and over the pass with stretches too narrow for two cars to pass, and the roadway is littered with rocks of all sizes that have fallen down from the banks above. It is laden with switchbacks and is beautiful the whole way.

I found a wide spot overlooking a stretch of the highway and stopped to take some photographs. While I was looking into the rangefinder, a car drove into my scenery. How on earth did the driver find the road? I wondered. Why did he have to stop here? The car pulled up to where I was standing, and despite my initial resentment, I found myself enjoying talking with the two men in the car, both of whom recalled driving over the pass before the new highway was built over Swauk Pass, which is hardly a steep grade by comparison. Like my wife, who is a native of the state, my new friends remembered being terrified while riding with their fathers over the pass in cars that now qualify as antiques. It was definitely not a trip for the faint of heart or the acrophobic.

I drove on in search of more photographs and solitude, and stopped just below the pass at a wide switchback and let the two

Burley Mountain Road

Facing page: *Mount Adams from near Trout Lake*

Left: *Mount St. Helens and Blewett Pass Highway*

Overleaf: *Blewett Pass*

men go around me. While I was carrying on my usual conversation with a camera—its light meter, to be specific, since it talks back to me in semaphoric signals when I put the wide angle lens on it—another car drove up, again with people who had traveled the pass way back when. I waited until they had continued on their way and was trying for my idea of what a switchback photo should look like, when a third car came along. I was astonished. It was a regular traffic jam.

I completed the photography, which was typically disappointing after being processed, and drove on down the southern side of the pass with the rest of the trip as solitary as I had hoped.

This is a pleasant and even exciting side trip off Highway 97, and the Forest Service is to be commended for preserving the road for the sake of nostalgia and scenery. It is much easier to find when driving Highway 97 from south to north because of a sign that says, in language even I could understand on the first reading: "Old Blewett Highway." There is also a Forest Service campground on the southern slopes on the outside of a switchback, and with views across the valley.

The Blewett Pass road is ten miles long, whereas the new highway over Swauk Pass takes 14 miles to cover the same distance. The latter isn't nearly as pretty, nor is it as much fun.

Washington Sketch:
GUARDIANS OF THE COLUMBIA

THE LOVE TRIANGLE, with two men competing for the affections of one woman, is a constant theme throughout human history. In Washington, one such triangle is memorialized in a legend told by the Indians along the Columbia River.

The story involves the three great volcanoes nearest the Columbia River: Mount Adams and Mount St. Helens in Washington, and Mount Hood across the Columbia in Oregon. These are the Guardians of the Columbia.

According to the Klickitat Indians, it was Tyhee Saghalie, chief of all the gods, who put the guardians there, and they say it was an act of harsh justice tempered by the melancholy of an old man whose sons took up arms against each other.

Long ago, according to the legend, Tyhee Saghalie and his two hot-blooded sons came down the Columbia from the Far North in search of a land suitable for the chief of all gods. After a long, hard trip, they came to the land beside the river where the waters narrowed and formed giant stepping stones for the gods to cross the river at their pleasure. When the white men came, they named these stepping stones The Dalles.

Saghalie and his sons had never seen a land so beautiful, but the two young men quarreled over it and Tyhee Saghalie settled the dispute by shooting two arrows from his powerful bow, one to the north and the other to the south. One son, Klickitat, followed the arrow to the north; he made the north his land and fathered a tribe named for himself. The other son, Wiyeast, went to the south and became grandfather of the Multnomahs, who lived beside the river named Willamette.

Tyhee Saghalie raised the mountains on both sides of the river to keep his sons apart, but remembering the cold of the Far North, he built none of them high enough to keep snow the year around. Next he built the most beautiful structure ever known, Tanmahawis, the Bridge of the Gods, so that his sons and their children might pass across the river in safety and that his family might not always be divided.

Then Tyhee Saghalie did another good thing, which brought about the destruction of his family. On the river lived a witch woman, Loowit, the ugliest of all the crones. But she could not be hidden away and ignored, for Loowit was in charge of the fire of the world. Although she was a witch, her heart was not hard, and when she saw how the little children suffered each winter from the wet cold, she made a gift of the fire to Tyhee Saghalie. His gratitude was without limit and he offered Loowit anything she wanted.

She asked to be made young and beautiful. Tyhee Saghalie made her the most beautiful woman in the world, and every young man who saw her desired her. But she paid them no attention. She was waiting for a husband who deserved such a beautiful and talented wife.

Then she met Tyhee's sons, Klickitat and Wiyeast. Both courted her. She could not decide between them for both were equally strong and handsome and powerful. The tribes soon were at war, and brother was set against brother.

Tyhee Saghalie destroyed the Bridge of the Gods so the people could not cross to hurt each other. But the fighting continued. This left Tyhee Saghalie both angry and sad, for he knew that to destroy the fighting, he must destroy the cause.

He put his sons, Klickitat and Wiyeast, to death, then slew Loowit, too.

Since he loved all three, the brokenhearted old chief turned them into mountains, the greatest mountains he had ever seen. Wiyeast became Mount Hood and Klickitat became Mount Adams. Because Loowit was so beautiful in life, he made her the most beautiful mountain in death. She became Mount St. Helens.

The rocks from the Bridge of the Gods are still there, beneath the backwaters of a dam. Until they were covered by a lake, the white men called them The Cascades.

And Tyhee Saghalie? He trudged back to the Far North and was never heard from again.

A telephoto view of Mount St. Helens from Burley Mountain

93

MOUNT RAINIER

NEWCOMERS to the Puget Sound basin are often puzzled the first time they hear the question: ''Is the mountain out?'' Where, they wonder, did somebody hide it? Does it have a den, or a condominium unit to sleep in? That is the way generations of Mount Rainier watchers have described the mountain because it is possible to live within 50 miles of it for weeks at a time and never see a trace of it. It is so huge that it attracts clouds and even creates them when conditions are right; its steep slopes force warm air upward and it cools into clouds.

Mount Rainier, although potentially dangerous since it is an inactive volcano, is undoubtedly the most popular piece of scenery in Western Washington and parts of Eastern Washington as well. It is nature's Beethoven's Ninth Symphony, and for decades Seattle and Tacoma Rainier lovers have argued over which city has the best view of the mountain.

One reason the mountain is so striking is that the other peaks around it in the Cascade Range seldom top the 8,000-foot mark. Mount Rainier stands 14,410 feet high and is,

Below: An early motoring party to Mount Rainier

Facing page: First ice of the winter in Mount Rainier National Park

to use a word in its purest definition, massive. It is broad all the way up rather than sharp-pointed.

The mountain is so stunning and the highways run so close to its base that most visitors to Washington consider their trip incomplete without a visit to Mount Rainier National Park. During most of the year the main highways through the park, Washington Highways 410 and 706, give us bumper-to-bumper traffic consisting of tour buses belching diesel smoke and cars laden with camping gear.

There are alternatives to this stampede: the Carbon River and Mowich entrances from the northwest corner. True, these approaches do not offer you the miles of stunning views of the mountain nor all the amenities of the lodges at Longmire and Paradise, but they do give you a bit of quiet and air clear enough for you to smell the forest. And they take you through some beautiful farmland en route to the park and through the picturesque little towns of Carbonado and Wilkeson.

Take Washington Highway 165 south from Buckley and you'll soon be in dense timber on a winding, narrow highway that crosses rivers and ravines on one-lane bridges. The only real town, in the sense that you can stop and buy food and gifts, is Wilkeson, which was a coal-mining town back in the days when coal was the major source of energy for industries. The town has gone through something of a revival during the past decade or so, and several of the old houses have been restored and look as though they were headed to Port Townsend or some other Victorian city, but stopped near Mount Rainier.

South of Wilkeson a few miles the highway forks, offering you the choice of taking the Carbon River entrance or the Mowich approach. The Carbon River route follows that river past a few summer homes and the inevitable clear-cut areas until the park boundary is reached. Immediately you are driving through forest that has never heard the sound of a logging truck. The only chainsaws heard are those used to clear fallen branches, or whole trees, from the highway. One of the first signs beyond the entrance is a reminder that no wood on the ground can be picked up. The forest there is totally natural.

The highway winds around the hillside just above the river bottom, occasionally passing a small lake or pond, then cuts away from the river into the dense forest to finally end at Ipsut Creek Campground.

This route is popular with the snowshoe and cross-country ski crowd early in the winter before the roads are closed by heavy snowfall. On my last trip there I passed several hunters patrolling the highway just outside the park boundary, and hadn't gone more than a mile inside the park before I saw three calm deer standing beside the road, virtually ignoring my car. They know where to go when war is declared every fall.

The other entrance on this route, the Mowich Lake approach, goes over a higher road that offers views of the mountain once you reach the top. There are a number of scenic turnouts on the way to the lake that show you the mountain and the more puny Cascade Mountains around the volcano.

Both routes have numerous marked trails for short walks to keep the trip from being a total sit-down experience, and you can pack a picnic lunch and eat at any of the turnouts or at the Mowich Lake Campground. It will give you a sense of freedom from the masses.

BUCKLEY TO EATONVILLE

THIS IS ANOTHER of those pleasant country roads that slow you down to a more sedate and safe speed while taking in some excellent views of Mount Rainier with farms and fences in the foreground.

This area was developed by timber and coal, the latter discovered here in 1874. Mining followed closely behind, and in 1904 a steam-driven electric plant was built and a town was founded nearby and named Electron. But in 1936 it almost became a buried city when a large earthslide engulfed part of the steam plant.

During the past few years the area has become popular with people who want the best of both urban and rural ways of life. Moderately wealthy families have bought farms along this route to raise horses and hay, often letting someone else farm their land on a share basis.

For a tour of this area, take Washington Highway 162 just south of Buckley and it will lead you through the villages of South Prairie, Crocker, Electron, and Kapowsin. Lake Kapowsin has several places suitable for picnics or fishing along the highway side, and a number of summer and permanent homes on the east side.

After a few sudden corners and jogs, the highway enters Eatonville. From there you can continue east on Washington Highway 706, which will take you into Mount Rainier National Park, or you can go north on Washington Highway 7 to Tacoma.

Washington 162 near Orting

Lake Kapowsin
summer homes

Washington Sketch:
THE FIRST ASCENT OF RAINIER

SINCE THE MIDDLE OF THE 19TH CENTURY, there has been a controversy over the name of Washington's highest peak. The Indians called it Takhoma ("mountain that is god"), but when Captain George Vancouver came through in 1792, on his expedition down Puget Sound, he named it for a friend. Tacomans have always preferred the original name and feel they have more right to its naming than Seattleites. In 1894, *Harper's Weekly* printed a story about the controversy with instructions on how to avoid the nomenclature problem while traveling in the Puget Sound area: In Seattle it must be Mount Rainier; in Tacoma, Mount Tacoma. On neutral territory, one might refer to "Mount Tacoma, or Rainier, as it is called" or vice versa. Then, with tongue in cheek, the magazine suggested compromise names, Taconier or Raicoma.

The debate resurfaces occasionally today, especially when the Board of Geographic Names plans a meeting somewhere in the West. But nobody disputes who climbed the mountain first or the fact that the two-man team was lucky to get off the mountain alive and with all body parts intact.

Attempts date back to a climb in the 1830s by Hudson's Bay employees, but it was two Americans who did it first, General Hazard Stevens and P. B. Van Trump, on August 17, 1870. An Englishman had started out with them, but he turned back after getting stuck on a peak.

Stevens and Van Trump hired the Mount Rainier pioneer, James Longmire, to guide them into the mountain's foothills, and Longmire in turn hired an In-

*P. B. Van Trump
back at his old
campsite*

dian named Sluiskin to guide them up the mountain. But Sluiskin proved to be an extremely reluctant guide, in somewhat the same way that National Park rangers today stop anyone trying the climb with only tennis shoes and a Thermos.

He led them into the lower reaches of the mountain, and they camped in a grove of timber the night before their summit attempt. Sluiskin spent most of that evening trying to talk them out of the climb. He told them Takhoma was an enchanted mountain, inhabited by an evil spirit, who dwelt in a fiery lake on the summit. No human being could ascend it and survive. Even the climb itself was impossible, he continued, because they would be killed by falling ice, tumble into a crevasse, or be stopped by cliffs of ice too steep even for mountain goats.

When he was unable to change their minds, he then asked for a "piece of paper" absolving him from blame for their deaths. This was the first known release form demanded by a guide on the mountain. Then he began singing his "dismal chant, or dirge," as Stevens wrote in "The Ascent of Mount Takhoma," far into the night while distant avalanches thundered.

Van Trump and Stevens struck out for the summit equipped with alpine staffs, creepers, a long rope, a brass plate inscribed with their names, flags, a canteen, and "some luncheon." They also carried gloves and green goggles for snow blindness. They were convinced that they could make the trip up and back in a single day, so they left behind their coats and blankets.

They had to abandon one route after Van Trump was struck by a falling rock, then had his alpine staff knocked from his hands by another. But they reached the summit before dark, faced with the unexpected problem of spending an extremely cold night on a peak without coat or blanket, and only a single lunch for each. While exploring the summit, they climbed down into a crater and found several jets of sulphur-smelling steam coming out of crevices on the north side of the crater. They decided to spend the night near one of the jets and keep warm "over one of Pluto's fires," the closest thing they could find to the fiery lake described by their guide. They built a wall of stones around the jet and found that "The heat at the orifice was too great to bear for more than an instant, but the steam wet us, the smell of sulphur was nauseating, and the cold was so severe that our clothes, saturated with the steam, froze stiff when turned away from the heated jet. . . . We passed a most miserable night, freezing on one side, and in a hot steam-sulphur-bath on the other."

The next morning they planted their flag and brass plate and began the descent. The trip down was made without serious incident until nearly back at base camp, when Van Trump fell on a snowbank and slid "like lightning 40 feet down the steep incline, and struck among some loose rocks . . . with such force as to rebound several feet into the air." He received several cuts and bruises and a deep gash on his thigh, but was able to walk. They found camp but Sluiskin wasn't there, although he had killed four marmot and dressed them out for roasting. Stevens cooked them, but didn't like the strong, disagreeable, doggy odor. While they were eating, Sluiskin returned and at first believed he was seeing ghosts.

That same year another team made it to the summit, and by 1892 a total of 38 people, including three women, had made the summit climb.

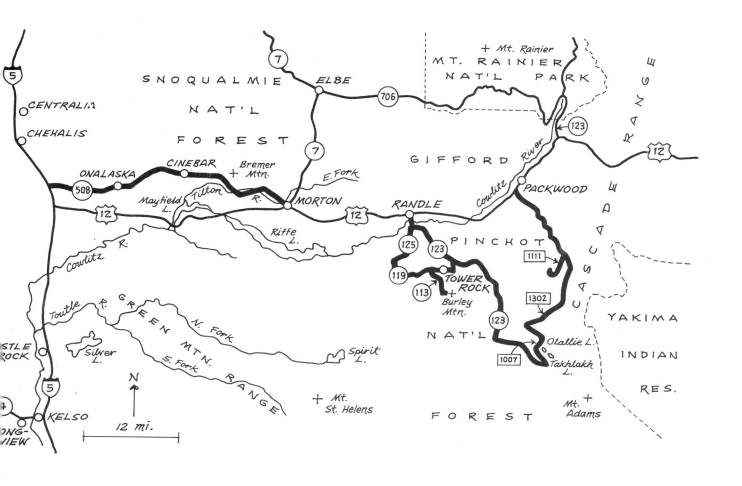

PACKWOOD TO RANDLE

MOUNT ADAMS sneaked up on me again while I was driving this long, looping trip south from Packwood toward the beautiful area around Takhlakh Lake. It was raining lightly as I drove south on Road 1302, a paved road that takes off into the wilderness just west of Packwood. When rain starts falling on your picture taking in Western Washington and up in the high country, it is best to keep going because sometimes the rain stops entirely and lets the sun through, or at the least gives you some special effects of light and shadow that a picture-postcard day might not offer.

At any rate, I kept driving, a little glum because of the weather but glad to be off the well-traveled US Highway 12 that goes over White Pass. I saw only one other backroader, a man in a pickup whom I passed while he was on a turnout kicking his tires.

Then, as unexpected as the crescendo in Haydn's Surprise Symphony to a first-time listener, Mount Adams, all 12,307 feet of it, appeared directly ahead of me as if by magic. It may have been in view before, but I immediately turned off onto Road 1111 and drove up the hill until I got an unobstructed view. Then I headed back to the south on 1302 and

101

Mount Adams from
Takhlakh Lake

*Forest Service Road
123 near Randle*

kept the mountain in sight for several miles, sunlight spotting its glaciers, and clouds appearing to be tied to its summit like a tail behind a kite. It was going to be my day after all.

The next stop was a spur-of-the-moment thing. I drove past Olallie Lake and the campground on its shore, but decided to go back and see what was there. It was fortunate I did because when I walked down to the lakeshore, I not only had a grand view of Mount Adams, I was also in the midst of a colony of tiny frogs on land and fat, squirming tadpoles at the water's edge working hard at becoming frogs. I had never seen this particular stage of a frog or tadpole's life before, and wished I had a contract with Walt Disney Studios or someone like that to preserve the moment. On the other hand, after watching them for a few minutes, I gave up on seeing any of them spring out of the lake onto dry ground with legs instead of tails.

This mass of hopping and wiggling creatures delayed me for a few minutes, but now I'm sorry I didn't pitch a tent and sit there as long as it took to observe the amphibian transfiguration.

Only a short distance on toward the mountain is Takhlakh Lake, which many consider the loveliest place in the whole Gifford Pinchot National Forest, named for the first chief of the National Forest Service. The campground there has produced as many color photographs as any lake in the mountains. It is only about three miles from the snout of Adams Glacier, which tumbles down the mountain, rumpled and crevassed. The appearance of the mountain changes constantly with the quality and quantity of the light, and although there are other things to see near the lake by taking short hikes, I doubt that I will ever get around to seeing them. Staring at the gently rounded slopes of Mount Adams from the lake is like watching a nature movie.

After you tear yourself away from this scene, you have a choice of going on south toward Trout Lake, described in another trip, or heading northwest to Randle and back to civilization. You will drive on gravel for a few miles on Road 123, then experience one of the nicest things that can happen to a backroader: you will still be in the wilderness with little traffic, but you will be driving on a smooth paved road complete with white lines down each side and a dotted line down the middle.

The trip on to Randle is uneventful after being right at Mount Adams's front door, but there is still another great trip you can make in two or three hours by turning off Road 123 at Tower Rock and following Road 119 to the Burley Mountain turnoff on Road 113.

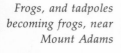

Frogs, and tadpoles becoming frogs, near Mount Adams

Sauk River on
Mountain Loop Highway

MORTON TO I-5

Facing page: *Mount Shuksan*

Left: *Mount Adams*

MORTON TO I-5

IF YOU FIND YOURSELF in Morton after backroading around Mount Rainier or down in the Mount Adams and Mount St. Helens backcountry, and you're still not ready for a major highway, swing off US Highway 12 and take Washington Highway 508 back to Interstate 5.

The highway leads past the outskirts of Morton, where you'll see more logging trucks than pickups parked in driveways on the weekend. This route follows the Tilton River several miles, then leaves it at Cinebar and begins climbing over Bremer Mountain. The mountain has been clear-cut of its timber, but that does open up the views. Then you'll drop down off the low mountain, negotiate a switchback or two, and you're back on a good, level highway all the way into Onalaska. From there you can go on to either Highway 12 or I-5.

This route takes only a little more time than the popular Highway 12, but the drive along the Tilton River and over Bremer Mountain is worth the extra time.

107

BURLEY MOUNTAIN

Mount Adams from Burley Mountain

THIS IS the kind of place that makes writers frantically flip through the pages of the desk thesaurus for new adjectives. I had to throw in the verbal towel even before I reached the summit and will try to restrain myself while describing the mountain.

It is on one of the many roads in Gifford Pinchot National Forest that are closed from the end of November until the end of June because of snow accumulation that keeps the road slick and threatens snowslides half of the year. Gates at the entrance are closed during this seven-month period for the safety of unbelievers.

But during the months this road is open, it definitely should be taken. From Randle you have your choice of two roads, both paved, that lead back to the small community of Tower Rock, huddled beneath a 3,337-foot jutting boulder of the same name. Road 123 is the more direct route, while Road 125 swings to the west a bit before connecting with Road 119 on the south side of the Cispus River. Road 113, which goes up Burley Mountain, swings off Road 119 and almost immediately begins climbing and switchbacking up the steep mountain. Unlike most Forest Service roads in the area, this one is sand and dirt, which makes it easier on the tires but also makes it more likely to be slippery in wet weather.

The route is a long seven miles up the mountain through dense trees until you emerge on a ridge cleared of timber. Here is one of the most spectacular views in the state. You can see Mount Rainier, Mount St. Helens, and Mount Adams clearly, looming up out of the lower Cascade Hills. Mount Rainier is about 15 miles away and the other two volcanoes are about 11 miles away. Mount Hood, across the Columbia River in Oregon, is some 50 miles away; it appears almost exactly between Adams and St. Helens.

You can stop on the first barren ridge, and if your car is low-slung or weak from the altitude, you should leave it here and drive no farther. The last pitch to the summit where the old lookout tower stands is very steep and littered with rocks that seem to be there to perform either of two functions: The rounded stones make you feel as though you're driving uphill on marbles, and the flat ones stand on end as if reaching for your oil pan. When you gain the top, there is no place for a large vehicle to turn around. So it is best to hike the last hill if your car can't turn around on a 9-by-12 rug. Under no circumstances should you try to pull a trailer up this mountain.

The climb to the lookout tower is worth the effort. Not only do you have a 50-yard-line view of the three major volcanoes in the South Cascades (sometimes the fourth, Mount Hood, is thrown in), you can see the peaks and ridges laid out below you in a series of lines that begin in shades of green, fade into blue, and finally recede into faint etchings of gray. It is a place you hate to leave once you arrive, even if you suffer from

mild acrophobia and worry about electrical storms blowing up before you can get down.

Chances are you will see the reverse side of Mount St. Helens here for the first time, and its 9,677-foot gently rounded summit lives up to its reputation of being the American counterpart of Japan's Mount Fuji. (As this book went to press, Mount St. Helens was erupting for the first time since 1857. As long as the volcano remains active, travel in some areas of Gifford Pinchot National Forest and all around the perimeter of the mountain will be curtailed. Check with the Forest Service or local law enforcement agencies before planning your trip.)

If you can stand on the summit of Burley Mountain and look at the four major peaks without giving them human characteristics, committing the unforgivable literary sin of the pathetic fallacy, you are a stronger person than I am. I stood looking at Mount Adams, dappled a bit by the sunlight, and thought it looked cheerful. Mount St. Helens, the perfect feminine cone, was demure beneath a cloud cover. Mount Rainier, its top hidden in the clouds, looked grumpy as if it had just slammed the door on an unwanted guest. Mount Hood, miles away but with its sharp peak elbowing its way into the scenery, was the brash cousin making its presence known.

The higher elevations of 5,310-foot Burley Mountain are favored by huckleberry pickers during late July and early September, and fortunately there is a road that continues south from the mountain along the highest ridge. This permits some free flow of traffic to prevent clogging all the way up the mountainside.

Perhaps with continued heavy use of the mountain, the existing road will be widened and improved before long. With such a beautiful view, and one of the few such views available in the area, it isn't difficult to envision the day when Burley Mountain will be an established public park. It would get my vote.

Washington Sketch:
THE APE MEN ATTACK

THE DEBATE still goes on over the existence of the Sasquatch, also known as "ape men," or simply "Big Foot." These creatures that are supposed to roam the deep forests of the Cascade Mountains are part of the legacy handed down to us from the Indians of the mountains who told the first white settlers stories of encounters with these giant, furry creatures. Since then, scientists have led expeditions into the forests, international Sasquatch conferences have been held, and photographs purporting to show the creatures have been exhibited.

One of the most famous Sasquatch happenings took place on the southern slopes of Mount St. Helens just below the lava maze called The Plains of Abraham. It was in 1924 and a group of miners were working in the area when, they said, a band of the hairy creatures charged them. One of the miners swore he was within 15 feet of a Sasquatch when he fired five shots from his revolver into it and it kept coming at him.

The miners fled to their cabin and spent a harrowing night. The creatures pelted the cabin with stones, and the black night was filled with their screams. The next day the men shot at another one and apparently killed it because the body tumbled into a canyon, which was later named Ape Canyon. The miners managed to escape back to civilization, and told their story in Kelso and Longview.

A posse composed of a few lawmen, a lot of loggers, and some reporters struck out for the Mount St. Helens foothills, and, like city-slicker deer hunters, "didn't see anything but got a lot of brush shots," meaning they fired at anything they heard or thought they heard. Surprisingly, when the posse gave up the hunt, nobody had been killed by stray bullets.

All through the years sightings have been reported, and plaster casts have been made of giant footprints found throughout the Cascades. One rather grainy and indistinct photo shows a well-endowed ape woman loping off into the brush. People have insisted they were kidnapped for brief periods by the creatures. Their detractors joke away such claims by saying it is an attempt to explain a two- or three-day drunk or some other disgraceful act.

In the interest of science and fair play, the Skamania County leaders decided to protect what they consider a unique natural resource, and County Ordinance 69-01 was passed on April 1, 1969, making it a felony to slay a Sasquatch to the tune of a $10,000 fine and/or five years in jail.

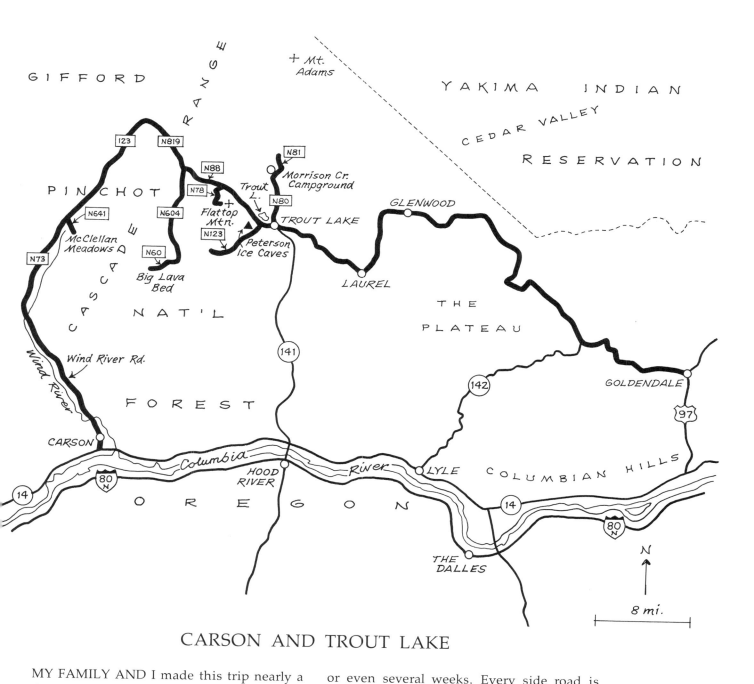

CARSON AND TROUT LAKE

MY FAMILY AND I made this trip nearly a decade ago, and I didn't return until I traveled for this book. Our memories of that initial trip consist of one accident, when a daughter's finger was mashed by a car door, and one night of camping in the rain. We knew it was a beautiful area even though we hadn't seen much of it on that occasion. But we didn't know how much we had missed.

This whole area between Mount St. Helens and Mount Adams deserves a week

or even several weeks. Every side road is worth a visit, even if it is a dead end, and there are many places that throw you off schedule because they are more beautiful or more interesting than you expected. So it is best to have no set schedule nor firm plans while wandering through here.

The most pleasant surprise was asphalt. In the past decade, nearly the entire loop trip from the Columbia River has been paved. Not the side roads, of course, but the major roads are in excellent condition, and the unpaved connecting link is good all-weather gravel road.

The drive east up the Columbia River Gorge from Vancouver on Washington Highway 14 prepares you for the backcountry driving. Unlike the Interstate across the river in Oregon, Highway 14 is crooked, narrow in spots, and tends to be more up and down than straight across or through. At the small town of Carson, turn north on the Wind River Road. This takes you into the heart of the Cascades, first past farms in the small valleys, then into the timber. The Wind River settlement has a large tree nursery and experimental station, and a fish hatchery, which is open for groups by appointment.

Continue north on the main highway and you'll come to an intersection. Take Road N73 north, and you're soon in the middle of the mountains, following the Wind River upward as it grows smaller and smaller each time you pass a feeder stream. Expect to see deer along the way, and unless you're there in the huckleberry season, don't expect to see many other cars. Several of the lower mountains pop up out of the timber occasionally, but the best is yet to come.

Parenthetically, the Forest Service has done a good job of installing enough signs at intersections so that you don't have to worry excessively about reading all the road numbers, although it is a good idea to double check your route occasionally.

Road in Gifford Pinchot National Forest

A few miles before the road climbs into the high country with the views of surrounding peaks and volcanoes, there is a short turnoff on Road N641 to McClellan Meadows. It doesn't offer much in the way of scenery, but does give us a reminder of one of the first federal boondoggles in the Pacific Northwest. You may recall that George McClellan was the reluctant general who gave President Lincoln fits of rage and despair during the Civil War. He also made innumerable cowboys miserable with his saddle design, which one cowboy told me was like riding astride a plank box.

In the Pacific Northwest McClellan is known for his expedition in 1853, under orders from Secretary of War Jefferson Davis (this was before the Civil War and Davis's presidency of the Confederate states), to look for a railroad route through the Cascade Mountains. But Davis told him not to look very hard. Davis wanted a southern route for the railroad through areas more likely to be proslavery than the northern territories. It would also economically benefit the existing southern states because the eastern terminus would most likely be in what became the Confederacy.

McClellan, then a captain in the Army, was just the man for the task. He dillydallied around Fort Vancouver until he at last had to move out or grow roots. McClellan Meadows is one of the places he camped en route north along the Cascades while trying not to find a pass suitable for railroads. True to his instructions, he didn't find a single pass over the Cascades.

This infuriated Territorial Governor Isaac I. Stevens, who had already found at least two passes, and Stevens wasn't one to sit around complaining when someone tried to discredit him.

Stevens, angry over McClellan's delays, meanderings, and negative reports, sent a man over Snoqualmie Pass in the dead of winter to prove the pass was practical. Not only did the solo traveler cross the summit with no problems, he turned around and

hiked back over it. Stevens made his point. Undoubtedly Stevens could have become a major American historical figure, but he was the very first officer killed in the Civil War. Some historians think the war would have ended much sooner had Stevens and McClellan exchanged places that day.

But the first railroad across the Cascades, the Northern Pacific, wasn't completed until 1887, after all railroad construction was slowed or halted entirely by the Civil War. In the meantime, Union Pacific and Southern Pacific were already in operation, and the Pacific Northwest had to wait until James J. Hill was able to forge several existing railroads into one and it opened for business in 1893, using the Stevens Pass route. That was a nice piece of justice, since the pass was named for the territorial governor. Understandably, no major pass was named for McClellan, and the short side trip off the main road to McClellan Meadows is no more exciting than McClellan's journey of nondiscovery.

But only four or five miles farther north, the scenery improves dramatically. When the road enters cleared country, a euphemism for logged-off, the peaks emerge, St. Helens to the west and Adams to the east with all the lower peaks in between. This logged-off area has the only unpaved stretch of road on this trip, and it doesn't last more than three or four miles before pavement appears again.

This is some of the best huckleberry picking in the state, and at one point there is even a paved and marked parking lot for berry pickers! This brings up a reminder, in case you should miss the signs: All berries east of Road 123 belong to Indians, under an agreement reached between the Forest Service and Indian tribes several years ago. Road 123 begins near the crest of the Cascades near the unpaved area you will drive through on this loop trip. Once you reach this area, it is best to assume that only Indians are permitted to pick the berries. There are thousands of acres of huckleberries elsewhere in this backcountry, so nobody should feel deprived. Also, during the height of the season, local residents offer them for sale at the small towns on the edge of the national forest.

Unless you are totally familiar with these roads, the major mountains have a disquieting way of suddenly appearing, almost as if they jumped out of the timber to unnerve you like Sasquatches are supposed to do. After you have been driving near them for several miles and you have about given up on seeing them at all, turn a curve or climb a gentle rise and there one will be, so near and so large that it is honestly startling. I'm sure I took the equivalent of an extra roll of film to make sure I got pictures of the mountains just in case they disappeared again into the trees and stayed there.

The most direct route from the crest of the Cascades is to join Road 123 north for about a mile, then take Road N819 south to N88, which heads toward Trout Lake. There is a variety of side trips to consider along this route, although only N819 is paved all the way back out of the forest. One side trip is on Road N604 south to Road N60, which takes you to the Big Lava Bed, a vast lava flow that the forest hasn't completely conquered yet.

Another side trip, on Road N78, takes you up Flattop Mountain, which has an excellent view of Mount Adams.

N88 intersects with N123 just outside Trout Lake, and a short distance west of the intersection is the Peterson Ice Cave, which locals used for their supplies of ice before the advent of electricity and refrigerators in the area. The cave is a walk-in type, and no matter how hot it is outside, take a sweater because it feels like you're entering an icebox.

Trout Lake is a pleasant town with an economy based on logging, farming, and tourism. It is the southern hub of the Gifford Pinchot National Forest logging activities, and it is only 22 miles from there back to the Columbia River at Bingen. The Forest Service has a ranger station on the edge of town, and you should stop in for suggestions on which side roads to take throughout the area. Nearly every road will lead you to something of interest, if nothing more than a new view of the surrounding mountains and Mount Adams. On my most recent visit, alone this time, unfortunately, I drove north of Trout Lake on N80 past a picturesque, decaying barn with Mount Adams in the background, with no particular goal in mind. Maybe I would try to drive to Bird Creek Meadows over on the Yakima Indian Reservation side of the mountain, or maybe I would try for the Cold Springs Campground with the Timberline Camp above it. It didn't make a lot of difference; I was only exploring, not going somewhere definite.

I chose Road N81 and drove to its end just beyond Morrison Creek Campground, although the road was very rough and deeply rutted in places, and I didn't average more than two miles per hour all the way above Morrison Creek. The road was dead-ended by a barricade of boulders and logs before its end at timberline, so I started hiking up toward the mountain, stopping occasionally to try for photographs of Mount St. Helens and Mount Hood. I had walked at least a mile when I met a young climber returning from the summit, alone and ahead of the rest of his party because he had forgotten his sunglasses and had a mild case of snow blindness. We chatted awhile, and he told me I had quite a distance to cover before the mountain "really opened up" for photos. So we walked back together and I had my first conversation with anyone other than the Honda in two days.

As I drove back toward Trout Lake, I saw the views of the mountain that I had been watching for all the way up. The road twisted and turned so much that I was driving with my back to the views on the way up. After several stops for more photos, I was back in the valley around Trout Lake wishing I had at least a week to wander around those mountains.

TROUT LAKE TO GOLDENDALE

AFTER YOU FINALLY tear yourself away from the Mount Adams backcountry, a nice way to leave the area is to go from Trout Lake to Laurel, Glenwood, and on east to US Highway 97 at Goldendale.

There are two roads from Trout Lake to Glenwood, but the best is via Laurel from the intersection on the northern outskirts of Trout Lake. The road is paved all the way,

and you and your car will need the rest after a tour of Gifford Pinchot National Forest. The road leads down a narrow valley with a few farms and ranches, then climbs up above the valley and over a ridge into more open country that has a worn-saddle and barbed-wire look to it. "Cowboy and logger country," a young man who lives in Glenwood told me.

*Klickitat River
Canyon and Mount
Adams*

115

Mount Adams occasionally appears over the tops of pine trees and is reflected in the small lakes that you pass beside the road. Laurel isn't really a town, more of an intersection where you turn north and wind around the meadows and clusters of trees until you reach the grocery store–post office–three-tavern town of Glenwood.

After you've been driving along the level basin for a few miles, the road suddenly dips down into the Klickitat River Canyon, which is difficult to see because of the thick trees. But a turnout takes you to a scenic point overlooking the winding river with Mount Adams peering over the shoulder of a lava butte directly ahead.

The road drops into the deep canyon, follows the river a short distance, and then begins climbing again, winding around the faces of the barren hills overlooking the river with several places wide enough for you to pull over and take in the scenery.

When I drove this route in August, there was a bumper crop of locusts, or grasshoppers, as we colloquially called them in my childhood. At first I couldn't figure out what was happening outside the car because it sounded like sleet was hitting the fenders and grill. A closer look showed that I was massacring hundreds of the leapers. They appeared to prefer the windiest and most exposed points along the canyon road, but I never got around to asking an entomologist why this was so. It was a hot day and I neglected to roll up my window while driving through them, and before I was back on level ground above the canyon, I had one locust and one hornet for passengers. Getting the hornet out of the car was fairly easy; I opened all the windows and he eventually found one. But the locust huddled on the floor out of sight until I stopped and began a search. After several unsuccessful attempts, I finally captured him with a cupped hand, then grasped him with my fingers and evicted him, only after he had spat on me.

Just north of Klickitat the road joins Washington Highway 142, which runs from Lyle on the Columbia River to Goldendale, and the rest of this trip is between wheat fields with an occasional sunflower farm. The odd thing I noticed about these hundreds of acres of sunflowers is that the sun was over in the western sky and the sunflowers were still gazing off to the east. I thought they followed the sun.

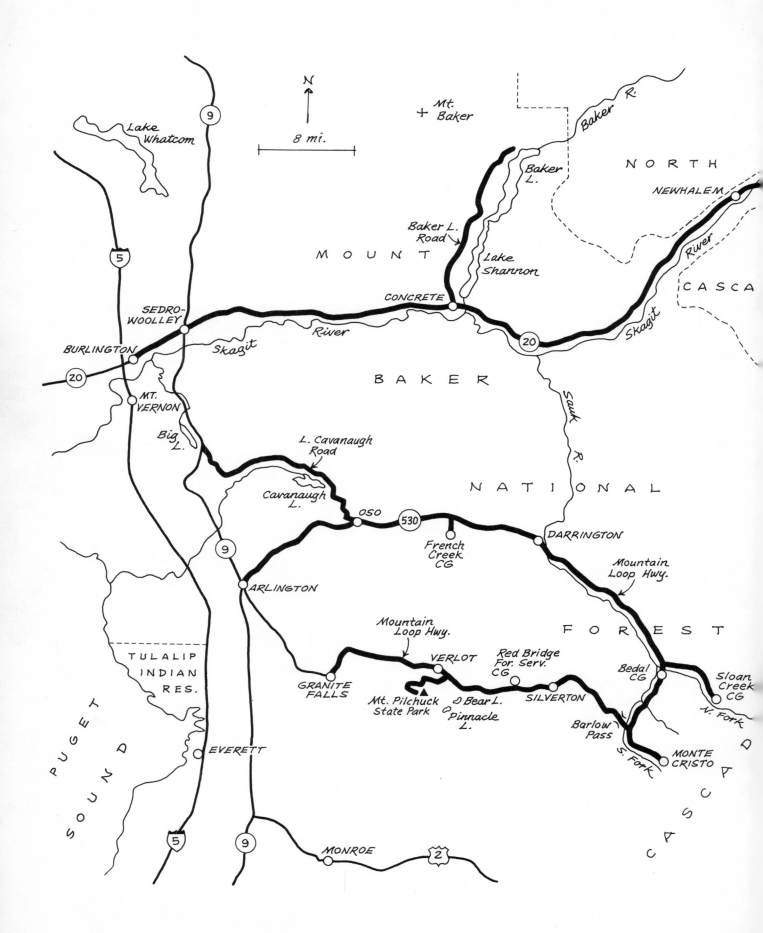

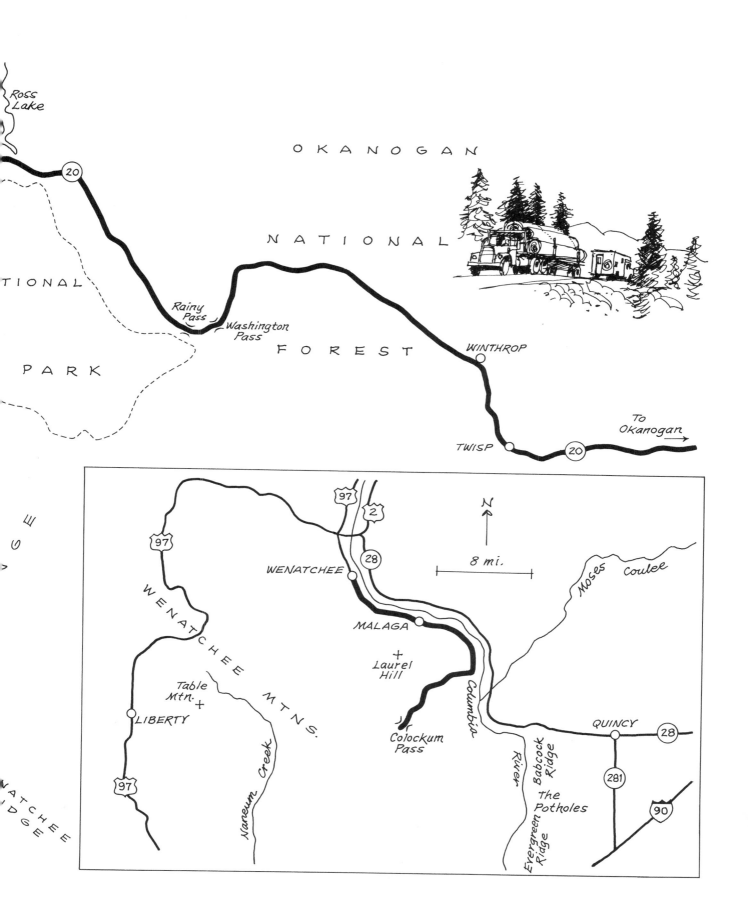

Ross
Lake

OKANOGAN

NATIONAL

20

TIONAL

PARK

Rainy
Pass

Washington
Pass

FOREST

WINTHROP

To
Okanogan

TWISP

20

97

2

97

WENATCHEE

28

N

8 mi.

Moses Coulee

W E N A T C H E E   M T N S.

Table
Mtn. +

LIBERTY

97

Naneum Creek

MALAGA

+
Laurel
Hill

Colockum
Pass

Columbia

River

Babcock Ridge

Evergreen Ridge

the
Potholes

QUINCY

28

281

90

NATCHEE
DGE

MOUNTAIN LOOP HIGHWAY

THIS IS the best trip available to the interior of the Central Cascade Range, and certainly one of the most beautiful loop drives in the state. It seems to offer everything but a desert. You follow three different river courses, run along the edge of the mountains, and at one point go over a pass into the very heart of the Cascades. Yet you are seldom more than 20 miles from a town.

Best of all, you have a variety of choices to make along the way. You have dozens of side roads to explore, campgrounds at regular intervals beside the rivers, good fishing, historic mining towns, and . . . well, you must try it. A warning: It is possible to make the loop in a day, but you'll regret it if you don't allow three or more days.

The highway came into being because of gold and silver mining along the North Fork of the Stillaguamish, where Robe, Verlot,

*Granite Falls fish
ladder*

120

Silverton, and Monte Cristo were built. During the 1880s and 1890s, Monte Cristo was the major mining area in the Western Cascades. The Guggenheims, Rockefellers, and other high-rollers in mining circles invested heavily in the mines, and built the town of Everett as a saltwater exit for the ore. The boom soon fizzled, leaving the remains of the towns. Only Everett, due to its good port facilities and logging, survived and grew.

The northern portion of the loop, from Arlington to Darrington, was built because of the logging industry, which began shortly after the turn of the century. The Darrington area was settled by loggers imported from the Carolinas, and it still retains much of its "tarheel" flavor with the accents of its inhabitants, fiddling contests, and bluegrass music.

The two highways heading east into the Cascades were connected later by a logging road that follows the Sauk River north into Darrington from the crest of Barlow Pass, which is one of the lower passes at 2,313 feet. Since the route has become so popular, the gravel road has been oiled more and more frequently, and one assumes it eventually will become a paved road as are the other two links.

From Granite Falls, take the Mountain Loop Highway north and you will soon cross over the North Fork of the Stillaguamish River on a bridge just above the falls. Cement steps lead down to the falls, and you can go down and stand beside the tumbling water and walk along part of the fish ladder, which was the longest in the world when it was built. Undoubtedly, someone by this time has built a longer one. No matter. It is a beautiful place with enough water noise to keep you shouting if you feel you have to talk all the time. Don't expect to see the migrating salmon and steelhead, though. They swim beneath the steel grate you walk on.

From here, the highway goes through timber and along the edges of farms till you reach Verlot, where there is a Forest Service ranger station to dispense information, and a store or two where you can stock up before continuing. Near the cluster of civilization is a road leading south to Mount Pilchuck State Park, a popular skiing area in the winter and hiking territory in the summer. All along the route you will see signs pointing uphill both ways to lakes, popular leg-stretchers usually no more than two miles off the highway.

If you don't feel like exerting yourself but would like to sit by a lake for a spell, try Bear Lake, which has a good road to within half a mile of it, and a paved trail (that's right) to its shore. Another two miles on a well-tended trail takes you to Pinnacle Lake above Bear Lake. Both give stunning scenery with a minimum of effort.

Only a short distance east of the Bear Lake turnoff is the Red Bridge Forest Service Campground. Nearby is an old mining tunnel that goes back into the mountain about 125 feet, and along the river are ruins of the old mining railroad that led from tidewater to Monte Cristo. Some gold panners report getting "colors" in this area, but none have claimed they struck it rich.

Silverton, the next town, has been saved from ghost-town status by summer dwellers who have kept the few remaining structures in a respectable state of repair, and added a few new ones.

Just down the road from Silverton is the site of a magnificent resort complex called Big Four Inn, which unfortunately burned in 1949 and was never rebuilt. A Forest Service campground is there instead, and a mile-long trail leads across the river on a bridge and into the mountains to caves beneath the snowfield on Big Four Mountain. They are called ice caves, although they are really packed snow, and vary in number from year to year, depending on the snow pack. They are created by the streams running beneath the snow.

The road splits at the summit of Barlow Pass. The northern route is a continuation of the Mountain Loop Highway. The southern fork takes you down to the ghost town of Monte Cristo, which is privately owned now. You will be charged a nominal fee for entering. The owners have restored several of the old buildings, and the town is in a picturesque setting with snow-capped mountains on three sides. For an excellent overall view of the town and the valley, hike up the Poodle Dog Pass trail a short distance, and take your camera.

From Barlow Pass, the Mountain Loop Highway picks up the South Fork of the Sauk River and follows it into Darrington. There are a number of campgrounds along the way, and at Elliott Creek a road leads off to the east and ends up in the mountains at the trailhead to Goat Lake. The hike is just over two miles to the lake, one of the most beautiful in the area.

Another pretty drive on logging roads—watch for trucks—is east from Bedal Campground. You will soon pass a thundering waterfall on the Sauk, where there is a parking area on a short spur road. This is the North Fork of the Sauk. Both forks join near Bedal Campground.

Follow the logging road all the way up into the mountains and you'll come to Sloan Creek Campground, where trailheads lead to a lookout tower or back into the Glacier Peak Wilderness. The road keeps going, and if you take logging road No. 308 to its end

rather than the 308A spur, you will come upon a magnificent view into the Cascades.

From Bedal, the main route takes you into Darrington, a colorful town that has a tendency to get rowdy on weekend nights. If you decide to visit a tavern for refreshments, it is best to do so quietly.

The remainder of the loop trip is down a broad valley with row-crop farms, hayfields, and an occasional Christmas-tree farm along Washington Highway 530. One of the best car-campgrounds on the trip is at French Creek. It is very large, the marked campsites are separated by brush and timber, and it is usually quiet at night. A gravel road leads from the campground and dead-ends on Boulder River, an aptly named stream that apparently doesn't have a smooth stretch in it. The trail is relatively level and leads past some elderly open-fronted wooden shelters. Just beyond the second shelter, and the prettiest one, the trail gains elevation to follow the edge of the canyon. Directly across from the trail are twin waterfalls that tumble down into the small river.

It is a short drive on west to Arlington, where you can continue on Washington Highway 530 to the intersection with Interstate 5, or turn on Washington Highway 9 and go north or south.

Below: *View across Stillaguamish River Valley en route to Lake Cavanaugh*

Facing page: *Liberty Bell Mountain*

*High meadow
near Hurricane Ridge
in Olympic National Park*

OSO AND LAKE CAVANAUGH

THIS MAKES a good side trip off the better-known Mountain Loop Highway and gives you a spectacular view from the top of one mountain range across the valley to another.

Oso is a small community and railroad siding on Washington Highway 530 east of Arlington. Almost immediately after the turnoff toward Lake Cavanaugh, the road narrows to go between a cluster of houses and the bank of the Stillaguamish River, then widens slightly and enters the forest. It is paved only a short distance and simultaneously becomes dirt and steep.

The steepest portion lasts perhaps three miles and finally emerges on the face of the mountain with a wide flat space to park and look back across the valley toward Wheeler Mountain. The road still climbs steeply for a short distance through the timber, then levels off and passes through a tall stand of second-growth timber before descending to Lake Cavanaugh.

The lakeshore has been turned into a summer-cabin city, and you have to drive nearly all the way around the lake before the road swings close enough to shore to get a good view. Then it cuts back into the timber to make room for cabins on the shore, and heads downhill again toward Washington Highway 9.

The last few miles of the road are paved, and pass small hay farms, berry farms, and a scattering of small cabins. Pilchuck Creek follows it a short distance, showing bleached boulders at low water.

The road enters Highway 9 at Big Lake. You can go north on Highway 9 into Sedro Woolley, or take Washington Highway 538 into Mount Vernon and catch Interstate 5 there.

Lake Cavanaugh

COLOCKUM PASS

IN THE INTRODUCTION I promised there would be no four-wheel-drive trips in this book, and there won't be. But when we took off over Colockum Pass nobody had told us you need tree-climbers to get all the way over it. Nobody told us because we didn't ask. But we are glad we tried it anyway.

Colockum Pass is on nearly every road map of Washington, and an acquaintance once gushed a bit over what a neat trip she had over the pass. So we drove from Wenatchee south along the Columbia River through Malaga with the barren hills to our right and the slack water of the Columbia to our left, then swung away from the river and up a narrow road that follows a ravine with stream into the hills. The road passes several small ranches, most of which are down in the ravine below the road, giving you a good view of tin roofs glinting in the sun and making the whole ranch complex look like a toy village of the kind you used to cut off the back of cereal boxes.

The ravine is a picturesque one that opens up into a broad valley with low timber, gates, and cattle guards. The pavement ends soon after entering the valley and the road is only infrequently graded, which forces you to slow down enough to admire the details of the broad landscape.

All the way up you are climbing slightly,

third gear in a four-speed transmission and sometimes second gear. Then the road comes to a "Y" with the arm to the right going through a gate and across a cattle guard. The arm to the left goes across a timber bridge and up an extremely steep hill. We stopped at the turnout on the steep hill for a view back down the valley and could almost see the Columbia River about ten miles away. After negotiating the loose rock and chuckholes of the hill, we drove up a modest grade for less than a mile and found ourselves in a rancher's yard with two big dogs standing at the car window looking at us. The road continued, but it had become parallel ditches leading off to the left and steeply upward, and a small sign on a post at the edge of the ranch yard told us that passenger cars could go no farther: four-wheel-drives only.

We saw a teenaged boy near the barn, but since the dogs had such a great interest in the contents of the car—us—we only waved, turned around, and headed back to the Columbia. We consoled ourselves with the advice given to backpackers when making a hike somewhere and back on the same trail: You see more by traveling a route both ways. And that is the truth. Otherwise, we wouldn't have seen three teenagers stealing gasoline from a county dump truck parked back at the end of the pavement.

*Broken landscape
near end of
Colockum Pass Road*

*Winthrop's western
theme*

*Whistler Mountain
on North Cascades
Highway*

NORTH CASCADES HIGHWAY

THIS IS ANOTHER of those trips where it may sound as if the backroads definition is being pushed to its limit, but Washington Highway 20 is still new enough as a cross-Cascade route that several people have yet to traverse it from the Skagit Flats to the Okanogan. And since it is the state's highest cross-mountain highway, there are still long periods of winter when it is closed due to the heavy snowfall. So when you plan your trip, plan it between June and November or December.

For about 160 of the 188 miles from Interstate 5 to Twisp, you have only one side road to contend with. That is the Baker Lake Road that heads north from the town of Concrete to dead-end up near Mount Baker at the end of Baker Lake. Otherwise you are committed to a route through the magnificent North Cascades National Park. That is the major reason for establishing the park; it is extremely remote and rugged country with no other access by highway. There was a great deal of opposition to completing the highway that formerly ended on the western slopes at Diablo Dam and on the eastern ones a few miles to the east of the small town of Mazama.

Obviously, since there are no towns or service stations for such a long distance, and most likely never will be due to the national park, you will want to be sure to have enough gasoline to make the whole drive. If you see a sign saying something about it being your last chance for a certain number of miles, believe it and stop to fill up. It will be a long hitchhike either way.

As mentioned above, the one side road off the highway is from Concrete north along the Baker River. This route is becoming more and more popular during the summer months, and since it is usually free of snow for most of the spring and through the fall, you might want to wait until the off-season to explore it. The reason it is popular is obvious; it leads back into the mountains with the river, and the backwaters of Baker Lake, frequently visible from the road. The Forest Service has campgrounds spotted along the route, but they are usually filled in the summer months.

Back on the main highway, this is one of the prettiest drives in the state on good highway. Once the high country is reached and the timber thins out, you will see the various peaks and subsidiary ranges of the Cascades jutting up high above you, and if you watch closely, you probably will see climbers working out on the sheer faces of mountains near the highway.

You will go over two passes, Rainy Pass at 4,860 feet, and Washington Pass, 5,250 feet. They are the highest passes on a major Washington highway, and snowbanks line the highway up here until well into the summer.

Once you start down from the mountains into the Mazama and Winthrop area, you will be in the famed Methow Valley where Owen Wister lived briefly and which he described in his classic novel, *The Virginian*. The valley has numerous streams of varying sizes meandering through hay meadows. The timber is thinner along the eastern slopes of the Cascades and the views of the mountains of the North Cascades are dramatic. This is one of the last places in the state where you'll see real cowboys, and each fall a few local ranchers band together for old-fashioned cattle drives when they move their cattle down from the high ranges ahead of the snow. A number of ranchers also operate packhorse strings to take fishermen and hunters into the high country during the summer and autumn.

Just east of Twisp you have a choice of going south past the town of Methow and catching the major Columbia River route, US Highway 97, or you can continue east on Washington Highway 20 to Okanogan.

Western Washington

VISITORS AND NEWCOMERS to the Pacific Northwest are usually amazed when they learn about Western Washington. It rains so much—more than 250 inches a year in places—that there are virtual jungles on the same latitude as Montreal and Quebec, and it is uncommon for snow to remain on the ground near sea level more than three or four days. While Spokane, less than 300 miles away, swelters in 100-degree temperature, Seattle and Tacoma residents are likely to wear sweaters in the evening. The reverse happens in the winter; while Spokane registers below-zero weather, Seattle is likely to be in the mid-50s.

Western Washington was one of the goals for travelers on the Oregon Trail in the 1850s, and a few relics of that great migration may still be seen. The state's largest cities are on the western slopes of the Cascade Range, clustered along Puget Sound. The mountains surrounding Puget Sound—the Cascades on the east and the Olympics to the west—are logging country, and most of the roads you will want to explore were originally built for logging or mining. Down in the foothills and valleys, the roads were built for farmers and small-town merchants. Many have been bypassed in recent years by the freeways that

*Facing page:
High in
Western Washington's
Olympic Mountains*

131

have slowly spread out from Puget Sound, while others that once were isolated now are major thoroughfares for people commuting to work.

Like other parts of the country, Washington has gone through the strange migratory pattern that originally brought farm and village youngsters to the city, nearly evacuating small towns and communities. Now people are moving farther and farther out of town and commuting to work, once again occupying the countryside. Thus, if you are traveling on a workday you must be prepared for late-afternoon traffic jams on some roads that an hour earlier appeared virtually deserted.

But there are seldom-used roads within an hour's slow drive of one of the major population centers. Some are surprisingly close to the cities—some even have views of the Seattle–Tacoma area.

You won't often get a feeling of solitude on Western Washington backroads, as you do on many backroads in Eastern Washington. There is usually a farmhouse or a mailbox within sight, never more than a mile or two away. There are a few exceptions, of course, such as when you drive through privately owned timberland near Hood Canal or in Southwest Washington.

Although Western Washington's rural areas may look much alike at first glance, there is an amazing variety between the Cascades and the sea, both in the general scenery and in the kinds of people who either settled areas or moved into them later. You can read every guidebook, every statistical report, and look at photographs of an area and still know less about it than after a brief, casual conversation with a person who lives there. This isn't New England, where people tend to be taciturn; if you ask someone in Western Washington about the place where he lives, you'll probably get a casual, sometimes funny description. And you'll remember that conversation longer than anything you read. So talk to the natives. They won't bite (although I suspect some of their big dogs will) and they're almost always happy to talk about their chosen home. Few people feel trapped by living in Western Washington.

Tree-covered slopes of the Olympics

*Fog muting the
early morning sun on
the Olympic Peninsula*

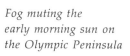

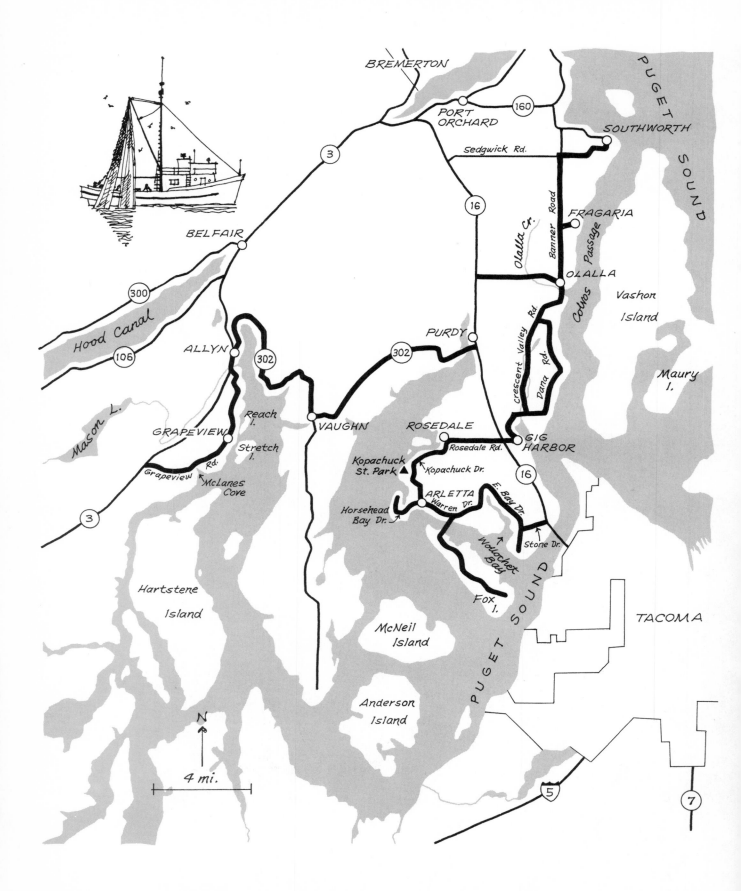

BREMERTON

PUGET SOUND

PORT ORCHARD

160

SOUTHWORTH

3

Sedgwick Rd.

16

FRAGARIA

Banner Road

Olalla Cr.

BELFAIR

OLALLA

Colvos Passage

Vashon Island

300

Hood Canal

106

Crescent Valley Rd.

Dana Rd.

Maury I.

ALLYN

302

PURDY

302

Reach I.

GRAPEVIEW

Stretch I.

Grapeview Rd.

McLanes Cove

Mason L.

VAUGHN

ROSEDALE

Rosedale Rd.

GIG HARBOR

16

Kopachuck St. Park

Kopachuck Dr.

ARLETTA

E. Bay Dr.

Warren Dr.

Horsehead Bay Dr.

Wollochet Bay

Stone Dr.

Hartstene Island

Fox I.

3

McNeil Island

PUGET SOUND

TACOMA

N

Anderson Island

4 mi.

5

7

GIG HARBOR TO SOUTHWORTH

WHEN THE WILKES EXPEDITION came through Puget Sound in 1841, Lieutenant Charles Wilkes discovered a narrow inlet that looked too shallow for his ships. He sent in a gig to sound the depth, then followed in the ship. The inlet opened into a beautiful little bay, which was sensibly named Gig Harbor.

A small town of the same name grew up around the harbor. It is movie-set beautiful and has become the home of artists, summer residents, and permanent occupants of the houses lining the shoreline. It is also the starting point of a nice alternative to the almost-freeway of Washington Highway 16. Go all the way around Gig Harbor to an intersection on the hillside north of town. Turn left (north) on Crescent Valley Drive, or continue east through the intersection and catch Dana Road, then turn north. Either will give you a pleasant drive past small farms, tall timber, and occasional summer homes. Dana Road also offers fleeting views of Colvos Passage and Vashon Island a short distance to the east.

The roads connect a short distance south of the store and dock of Olalla. Olalla Creek meanders down from the hills west of the Sound and through a wide valley, then empties into Puget Sound beneath a high bridge. It is a picturesque spot and one of the few places along this stretch of the Sound where you can stop at water's edge. The rest of the waterfront either is privately owned or the road goes behind bluffs too steep for roads.

At Olalla you can turn back to the west and catch the main highway, or you can turn sharply to the right and up a hill staying on Banner Road. The latter takes you to the turnoff to Fragaria, another small community clinging to a creek bank and steep hills above the Sound. Once you get to Fragaria, after driving down a steep road that descends into the darkness of a rain forest before leveling off, you won't find much to do other than turn around in someone's driveway and leave. Fragaria is tiny and crowded.

Both Olalla and Fragaria date back to the early years of the century when Puget Sound towns were served by what was called the Mosquito Fleet, several small passenger and cargo boats that would stop at any town or dock where passengers or freight could be picked up. The boats were privately owned and competition was stiff between the companies until more roads were built and the Washington State Ferry Commission took over most automobile and passenger traffic. Only one member of the Mosquito Fleet is still in commission, the *Virginia V*, a craft popular with maritime-history buffs.

Banner Road continues due north through timber and small farms and connects with Sedgwick Road. Turn right, toward the Sound, to reach the Fauntleroy–Vashon Island ferry at Southworth. The road continues on around the bluffs and ends in Bremerton.

Rain on Puget Sound

GRAPEVIEW

I FUMBLED MY WAY into Grapeview and out again without knowing where we were going. I thought we were traveling from Gig Harbor to Kopachuck State Park, then up to Belfair and around the inside of the Hood Canal hook. So certain was I of the route that the map was put away and we drove west on Washington Highway 302 and soon reached the salt water of, I was certain, Hood Canal's southern shore. It looked like Hood Canal with the still water, tideflats, and private homes lined along the beach between the highway and high-tide mark. So when we came to a town with a left turn on a narrow road, that was good enough for me. Although the sign indicated Grapeview was next, I assumed they had added a town since my last visit, and I pressed onward.

Luckily, it was a pretty drive. The road dipped down on the bluff far enough so that occasionally we could see the water, and the deep shade from the Douglas fir and alder trees kept the drive a cool one. I saw enough private-property signs to believe it was Hood Canal, since the private-property concept is more deeply ingrained along the canal than in most other parts of the country.

Odd, I thought, when I noticed a sign, off to the left, for Treasure Island. "Never heard of it," I muttered in that tone of voice used by those who believe any subject of which they are ignorant is obviously of no importance. But I drove down the short road and saw a bridge with a chain across informing wanderers like us that it was a private club. I pulled to the side of the road and prepared to walk over to a low bank that had a view of the bridge, but was brought up short by a no-nonsense no-trespassing sign.

We wandered onward, finally seeing salt water again beneath a bridge that we later found crossed McLanes Cove. But this was after we passed a store that we eventually learned was Grapeview. I duly stopped to take photographs of the cove, and drove onward hoping to reach Tahuya soon and buy a cold soft drink. We gained perhaps a hundred feet of elevation and found ourselves in the midst of a Christmas tree farm, a common crop in that area because the soil, mostly glacial droppings, isn't rich enough to support sustained-yield commercial timber crops. In the same area we passed signs warning off "brush cutters," the local terminology for those who harvest fern, salal, and similar wild plants to sell to funeral homes and other firms needing fresh greenery.

We blundered around a bit more before we reached a busy highway where cars and campers shot past as if they knew where they were going. We didn't. Eventually we wound around and arrived back at "start," which was Allyn, and went to Tacoma.

Later we learned where we had been. Although we didn't see a single vine, the area was named Grapeview because lots of grapes were grown in the area and it once supported a winery. Treasure Island used to be called Reach Island and still is on most maps, but the real-estate developers that took over the island didn't think Reach had the proper zippy sound. So they plagiarized Robert Louis Stevenson. The other small island, named Stretch, is nearby and makes one wonder if an exercise fanatic named them.

Typically, not once during the trip of discovery did I ask for directions. It is one thing to be lost and ask directions to where you hope to go. It is quite another to have made a 30-mile trip and then ask where you've been. In fact, after completing this book I decided that if I had asked directions every time I had been at least a little lost, all over the state people would be talking about that tall guy in a tiny car who walked in and asked: "Where am I?"

Like the other trips on which I was lost— none so completely as the Grapeview loop— it all worked out. In this case, I added to my collection a trip that I recommend as an antidote to the heavy traffic on Washington 3 between Bremerton and Shelton.

ROSEDALE, KOPACHUCK, AND FOX ISLAND

THE FIRST TIME we visited Kopachuck State Park, it was winter and only a handful of visitors were braving the gloomy day that threatened rain. The next time, several years later, was on a hot, sunny summer day and the parking lot was full and the gravel beach crowded. But the park is so large that it was possible to find a picnic table away from the scattered crowd.

A picnic lunch at Kopachuck is a pleasant interlude while traveling the loop route from Washington Highway 16 just south of Purdy and around the shore of Carr Inlet. The easiest route is to follow the signs off Highway 16, which lead you to Rosedale. Turn south at Rosedale, cross a broad tidal flat with a small creek running through it, and Kopachuck State Park is your next stop.

From there, the road leads down to Arletta, a pretty town on a high bank overlooking Hales Passage between the mainland and Fox Island. The area is a popular place for scenery lovers who don't mind commuting to work a few miles away in Tacoma, but it is still possible to park and share the scenery with them, which may include magnificent views of Mount Rainier. A turn west at Arletta takes you to Horsehead Bay, a calm and shallow bay ringed with houses and boats.

A short distance out of Arletta is another turnoff on a bluff with a view across to Fox Island. On a good day you can also see Mount Rainier. The road immediately drops down and a right turn takes you to the bridge connecting Fox Island and the mainland. It is a popular spot for scuba divers and boaters, and on the island side is a parking lot from which boats can be launched into Hales Passage. On those rare good days, Mount Rainier looms up above the passage and the island, making the trip worthwhile.

Unfortunately, there are no places with views on Fox Island for the casual visitor, but there is a small shopping center near the bridge for a soft-drink stop.

From the bridge, you can follow the road on around the peninsula, taking a jog around Wollochet Bay, or you can follow the signs to Gig Harbor, which will put you back on Highway 16.

This is a heavily populated area in spite of the backroad feeling you'll get, and there is a maze of streets throughout the series of little peninsulas, bays, and islands. In case you don't have a detailed map, here is the route I took, although nearly every road takes you somewhere interesting:

From Washington Highway 16 go west on Rosedale Road to Kopachuck Drive and Kopachuck Park. Continue south on the same road and it swings around and runs into Horsehead Bay Drive at Arletta. After making the Horsehead Bay trip, return to Arletta and go east on Warren Drive to the Fox Island bridge. After Fox Island, go north on Warren Drive and then around Wollochet Bay and south on East Bay Drive to Stone Drive, which takes you back to Highway 16 near The Narrows bridge. Here you can go across to Tacoma, or north back toward Bremerton.

Kopachuck State Park

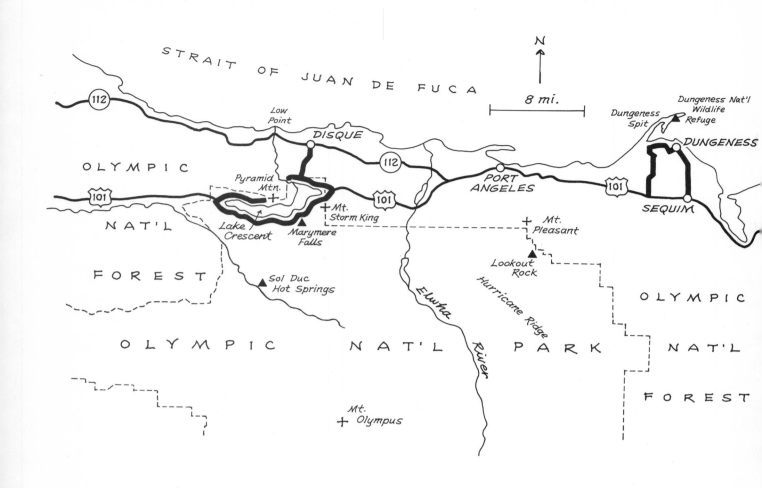

LAKE CRESCENT

THERE ARE SOME PLACES in the world with such a subtle beauty that it is virtually impossible to explain in words, and even photographs fail to catch the total visual impact. Lake Crescent is such a place.

True, US Highway 101 runs along the entire southern shore, and it is a rare weekday that five logging trucks can't be seen and heard every hour, plus hundreds of cars, campers, and motor homes. Since the mountains drop sharply off into the lake, the highway is very narrow and very crooked, and turnouts are few on that side.

Fortunately, a side road leads around both ends. On the eastern end, a road follows the lake around the northern shore and meanders on west a short distance

before turning away from the lake and heading northwest to connect with Washington Highway 112.

On the western end, another road follows the shore about a mile before dead-ending at a trailhead that leads to the top of Pyramid Peak, where an abandoned World War II lookout cabin still stands.

But what a lake! Seen from any angle, it is a postcard scene with mountains rising up from its shore: Storm King, Pyramid Mountain, and several lesser peaks. Mornings and evenings are frequently calm, and during cooler weather your reflections won't be butchered by the speedboats that carve up the mirrored surface during the hot summer months.

On the southern shore, a trail leads off from Lake Crescent Lodge to Marymere Falls. If you can walk to the store, you can walk to the falls. Only a few yards back into the virgin forest and you're out of sight and sound from the busy highway.

Although US 101 doesn't qualify as a backroad, you will have to travel it at least the length of the lake to get some of the best views. Otherwise, you can stay on the northern and eastern ends and wait for the view to change. And it will. If you should happen to be staying in one of the lodges National Park concessioneers operate, be sure to get up before dawn so you can watch the various moods of the lake change and unfold as the sun climbs over the Olympics. Evenings are equally beautiful.

*Evening on
Lake Crescent*

Right:
Territorial Governor
Isaac Ingalls Stevens

Facing page:
Olympic rain forest

Washington Sketch:
GOVERNOR STEVENS'S PARDON

IF THE COMIC-OPERA TEAM of Gilbert and Sullivan had written for Washington Territory audiences during the 1850s, they probably would have devoted one of their satirical operas to the shenanigans involving Governor Isaac Stevens and Judge Edward Lander, chief justice of the territory. Typically, this bit of silliness occurred at a time when Washington Territory was in danger of going back to the Indians by default.

It happened in the winter of 1855–56, the "blockhouse winter," so called because that is where a lot of settlers holed up during the Indian Wars that swept the Puget Sound basin that winter. The wars weren't much as wars go, except to those involved in them. History treats the wars as more of a footnote than an occasion.

But they were serious business for both Governor Stevens and Judge Lander. Stevens's militia was having no luck chasing the Indians, who had long been experts at hit-and-run tactics—attack and run and hide in the deep forests.

Stevens was very frustrated, and when a powerful man is frustrated, he looks for someone to attack. In this case, it wasn't hard to find a target for his anger. The Olympia and Southern Puget Sound area was dotted with farms owned by former Hudson's Bay employees who worked at the Fort Nisqually

Altoona

post. They had stayed in the area with their Indian wives and families rather than returning to England or going up into Canada after the US–Canadian boundary question was settled and the Hudson's Bay Company evacuated.

Stevens also noted that these settlers were not disturbed by the Indians, mainly because the Indians wouldn't attack their own relatives, the settlers' wives.

Stevens ordered them into the blockhouses with the rest of the farmers, who had gone inside for their safety. Most refused to go. Stevens ordered them arrested, but since they had committed no common crime, he had to declare martial law in the county in which they lived, Pierce County. He did so and they still refused. He had the militia pick them up and haul them in, and announced he would try them in a military court.

Lawyers immediately tried to get them released from the jail in Steilacoom. The presiding judge was ill, so Judge Lander was asked to come down from Seattle and hear the arguments. Lander at that time was commander of Company A of the militia, and he left his post without permission from the governor. He went to Steilacoom and opened court in defiance of Stevens's martial-law proclamation.

Stevens ordered a detachment of soldiers to Steilacoom to arrest Lander. He and his clerks were taken to Olympia and Lander was charged with being AWOL. Since he was chief justice of the territory, he was soon released and he set about opening court in Olympia, the county seat of Thurston County. In order to prevent that, Stevens placed that county under martial law, too. Hoping to put an end to the matter, Stevens released three of the five settlers he had placed under arrest, but kept two to be tried in a military court.

This wasn't good enough for Judge Lander, who was understandably smarting from being arrested. He opened his court to prove that civil law was still functioning, then ordered the arrest of Governor Stevens for contempt of court because he had refused to recognize Lander's court. Lander sent a marshal after Stevens, but when he came face to face with the governor the marshal backed down and returned alone.

This didn't make Stevens happier. He sent a militia company into Olympia with orders to bring Lander in. Lander heard they were coming, quickly adjourned court, and hid in the law office of a friend. The militia tracked him down, kicked in the door, and hauled the judge off to a nearby post where he was held in "honorable custody." Stevens eventually released him so he could hold court, but Lander was still fuming and continued his case against Stevens for contempt.

Stevens, preoccupied with other matters, had an attorney appear in court on his behalf and paid the $50 fine.

So far as everyone was concerned, the matter ended there. Little was heard of Lander afterward, and Stevens was killed in the Battle of Chantilly in the Civil War.

However, around the turn of this century a clerk rummaging through old territorial records came across a document signed by Governor Isaac Ingalls Stevens. It stated that Isaac I. Stevens, as territorial governor, had pardoned Isaac I. Stevens, convicted of contempt of court. The document was dated only a short time after his counsel had paid the $50 fine.

SEQUIM—DUNGENESS SPIT

THE OLYMPIC PENINSULA is noted for its beautiful scenery and its torrents of rain that make it one of the wettest spots in North America. The Hoh Rain Forest has an average of 140 inches of rainfall annually, and over on the coast itself there are years with more than 200 inches. But right in the middle of this constant showerbath is Sequim, the driest spot in Western Washington and one of the driest places on the West Coast. Its rainfall averages only 16 inches a year.

Meteorologists can explain this in all sorts of complicated ways, but perhaps the simplest is to say that Sequim is in a "rain shadow." The Olympic Mountains surrounding it catch all the incoming rain, except the occasional shower that manages to get over the barrier.

Consequently, farmers there have to irrigate while watching rain clouds dumping their loads all around them. Irrigation is such a big deal there that when the ditches were dug back in 1896, a festival was held for the occasion, and every second weekend of May the Irrigation Festival is still held there.

With such balmy weather as a selling point, real-estate salesmen have attracted retired couples by the score to the area, and much of the land that was once irrigated now is subdivided into building sites, or lots with small houses already built on them. These housing developments are drawing retired people from all over the country, from Long Island, New York, to Southern California.

The area makes an interesting side trip off US Highway 101. Just north of Sequim the road goes between—and through in some cases—gigantic heaps of dirt and gravel that look as though a bulldozer operator went off his rocker and started piling it up. This was actually caused by one of the Ice Age glaciers emptying its pockets, so to speak, when it reached its southern destination.

Out beyond this are the Dungeness flats, low marshy land around the Strait of Juan de Fuca. When you reach the general store and community hall of Dungeness, turn west and follow the signs to Dungeness National Wildlife Refuge. This will take you to the campground inside the wildlife refuge, where you can either camp or park while strolling down a road to the viewpoint overlooking Dungeness Spit.

This is the largest such sandspit in the country, some say, and it is still growing as sand is swept onto it from the straits. The spit (terrible name for something, isn't it?) is seven miles long. If you're a walker or hiker, you can make the trip out to the end of the spit and back in a day's hike. Or you can walk out only a short distance and marvel at the ten-foot-high piles of driftwood strewn along the strait side, and the calm, flat beach on the bay side.

You can either retrace your route back through Dungeness or follow signs from the campground that will take you to Highway 101 between Sequim and Port Angeles.

Dungeness Spit

HOOD CANAL occupies a special place in the memory of anyone who has ever spent more than 24 hours on its still shores. Of course it isn't a canal at all; it is an 80-mile-long arm of Puget Sound that cuts straight south, then hooks back to the east and turns northeast. It is narrow, shallow, and incredibly beautiful no matter from which side you approach it. It is noted for water warm enough for swimming, especially near the beaches, and for oysters, clams, shrimp, and silence.

Relatively busy highways follow its outside shores, but for a solitary trip with views of the Olympics most of the way, take the inside route. From the canal's southern end, take Washington Highway 300 from Belfair toward Belfair State Park and Tahuya. It is a narrow paved road all the way to Tahuya, where the canal takes its bend and heads north to Puget Sound. Except for Belfair State Park, there are no places where you can stop and walk down the beach since dwellers along the canal, of which there are hundreds, exercise their territorial imperative quite strongly. You can look at the beach with views across the usually calm water to the far shore from the roadway, but that's all.

The road follows the coastline faithfully most of the way, and if you leave on an early morning outing, you will probably see the fog that is characteristic of the canal. It quickly lifts and is burned off by the sun, leaving still waters reflecting the Olympics to the west.

Tahuya is a small resort town with only a few places of business, and just beyond it the road appears to enter a dark cave, actually dense timber. From here on to Dewatto you are on an honest-to-goodness backroad. It is steep in places, consistently narrow but with numerous wide spots at the bends where you can park to admire the views of the Olympics. As before, nearly all of the property along here is privately owned, and every road, trail, or path has a sign on it some-

where telling you to stay away. The road continues along the steep contours of the headlands, and finally straightens out after about eight miles and shows some sign of being maintained. Then it rather abruptly ends at a T-junction. Take the left turn back toward the water, and at the bottom of the steep hill, you will arrive at the Dewatto Creek tideflats. Take the road off to the left again, and it will lead you to the ghost town of Dewatto.

No stores function there now, and some of the buildings show signs of extreme wear, which adds to the romance of the area. One historical reference to the area indicates the Indians stayed away from Dewatto, but whatever the cause it doesn't apply today. Perhaps, as one scenery lover suggested, it was an effort on the Indians' part to keep tourists out. They were unsuccessful. More

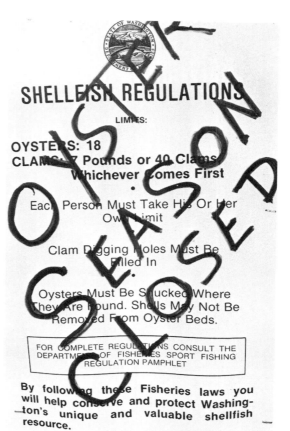

Shellfish regulations
sign stapled to
a post, near
Hood Canal

145

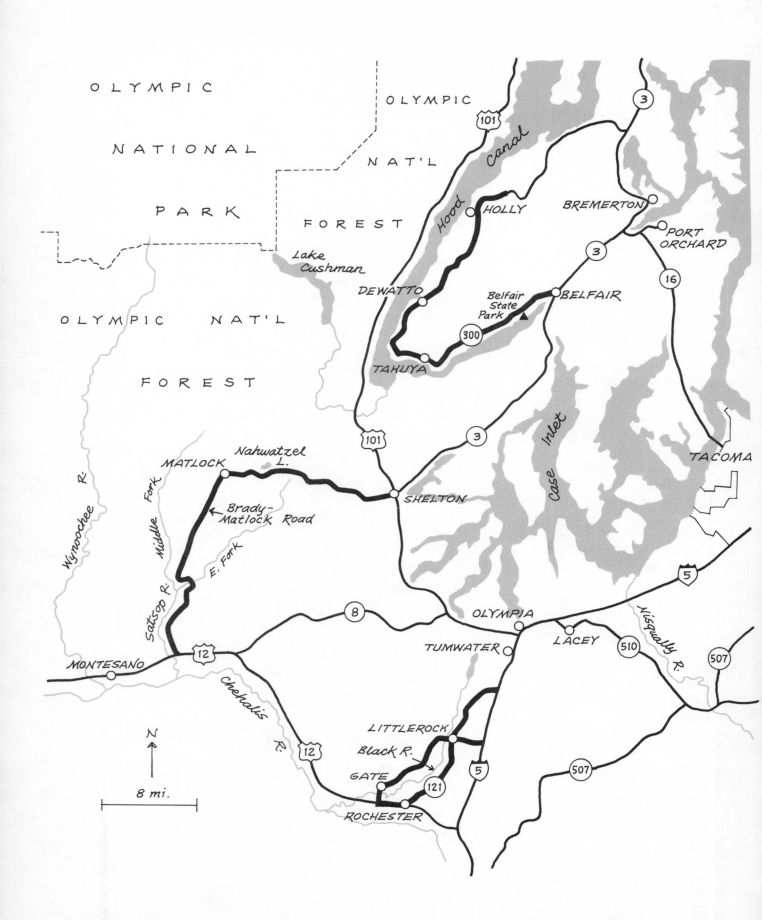

and more summer homes are appearing, even though it is so remote.

Beyond Dewatto the road leaves the shore and climbs up out of the old-growth timber and into an area that was logged off many years ago and has since been reseeded with beautiful small trees. The blacktop road is washboardy and sometimes seems sunken because the banks along it are so high.

Then you descend a winding hill back toward the canal with the Olympics again framing the scene, and the good road takes over. You can take a left turn at the bottom of this hill and visit the summer-home town of Holly, but you won't find a public park there. The main highway takes you to Seabeck, along Puget Sound's Dyes Inlet, and into Bremerton.

HOOD CANAL

Hood Canal and the Olympic Mountains

AS NOTED EARLIER, there are few backroads on the Olympic Peninsula. The majority of the land is in the Olympic National Park and roads in it are nearly always busy and dead-end at a trailhead or busy parking lot. Keeping a personal vow to give you no dead-end roads without a very good reason (such as getting lost on one and not wanting to waste the experience), there are few Olympic trips available. However, this shouldn't prevent you from exploring the Hurricane Ridge Road, which leads you from Park headquarters in Port Angeles to beautiful meadows above timberline with views of the mountains. You can also go up the Hoh River to the famous rain forest by following US Highway 101 along the coastal side. Still another popular route near Lake Crescent is south to Sol Duc Hot Springs.

For that matter, the whole length of US Highway 101 along the western, northern, and eastern edges of the peninsula is one of the most scenic drives in the state. But the presence of thousands of cars and RVs hardly qualifies it for a backroad designation.

So I had to be content with a relatively short trip from near Montesano, on US Highway 12, taking a backroad north to Matlock, then east to Shelton. It is a pleasant drive on a two-lane paved route with frequent signs telling you the speed limit is 45 miles per hour. I don't know why the road engineers limit the speed, but I do know I wouldn't care to drive any faster because it is a rough piece of pavement all the way around.

Turn north off Highway 12 at the Schafer State Park sign on Brady–Matlock Road. It follows the Satsop River Valley north through farms and near tree farms including the Weyerhaeuser Company's Clemons Tree Farm, which was the first commercial tree farm in the nation.

Much of the route is an asphalt-paved tunnel that passes between and beneath the tall second-growth timber, especially beyond the small town of Matlock. It is possible to turn west from Matlock and drive up to Camp Grisdale, on the edge of the Olympic National Forest. The last family logging camp in the state, it is owned by Simpson Timber Company. Another road, encountered on the way to Grisdale, leads over into Aberdeen.

East of Matlock is an occasional view of the southern end of the Olympic Mountains, which by now have dwindled down to a series of low ridges.

As with much of Western Washington, this area was first penetrated by loggers and logging railroads. Roads came along later almost as an afterthought. It is conceivable that there are still hundreds of square miles no man has walked on in Western Washington, although timber cutting is gradually moving into all the virgin timber remaining outside the protection of national parks and wilderness areas.

Much of the timberlands originally belonged to railroads as compensation by the federal government for building the rail lines into the West. Many were given alternate sections of land all along the route to sell or do with as they pleased. Some such land was sold off to timber companies. This was the case with Northern Pacific, which sold several million acres to the Weyerhaeuser interests. Other timber companies came along later and bought the land from either the federal government or Indian tribes.

Some subscribed to the "cut it and cut out" way of doing business by taking the best timber, then selling the stumpland for whatever the market would bear. But Weyerhaeuser, Simpson, Pope and Talbot, Crown Zellerbach, and a few others held on to the land, and the other companies followed Weyerhaeuser's lead in continually renewing their holdings, treating timber like a crop that is to be harvested, then replanted.

The Matlock area was quite wild until well into the middle of this century. Like most timber areas, it was burned over several times through the centuries by forest fires. A few have threatened to completely wipe out the residences in the foothills, and one did take some buildings from Matlock when it was primarily a railroad junction for Simpson Timber Company trains. The company still has a logging railroad you will see occasionally, bringing logs in from Camp Grisdale and other locations up against the Olympic National Forest. You will also see a few small lakes, plus the resort and summer-home lake named Nahwatzel. The road ends just outside Shelton at an intersection with US Highway 101.

Old wellhouse abandoned on farm near Matlock

THE MIMA MOUNDS

*Farm in the middle
of the Mima Mounds*

FEW NATURAL FEATURES in Washington have caused more theories to be advanced— but no solid facts—than the Mima Mounds just outside the small farming town of Little-rock. These dirt and gravel pimples from two to six feet high on the earth's surface are almost as difficult to photograph from ground level as they are to explain. In fact, they are best viewed from the vantage point of a low-flying small plane early or late in the day when shadows help define them. Of course, they can also be seen and appreciated from ground level.

One way to reach these strange phenomena is to take the Interstate 5 southbound exit marked South Tumwater–Tenino just south of Olympia and Tumwater, and follow the signs to "Old 99" Highway south. The mounds appear after you have traveled about eight miles.

A more direct route from I-5 is at the Littlerock exit farther south. Go straight through Littlerock and follow Washington Highway 121, which leads you almost immediately into the mounds, then past Weyer-haeuser Company's nursery, where up to 60 million seedlings are laid out in long rows stretching toward the horizon.

All through this area you'll see the Mima Mounds, which have rendered most of the land unfit for anything other than cattle grazing and scientific study. The area has been preserved, first by a 548-acre purchase by the Nature Conservancy and now by Registered Natural Landmark status from the National Park Service. There are around 900,000 mounds, according to one count, and the debate and speculation as to their origin go on and on.

One scientist insists they were built by a colony of gophers. Another says it wasn't just ordinary gophers, but giant gophers that have since departed the earth. The first settlers in the area assumed they were Indian burial grounds, but had to give up their treasure hunt after every attempt at digging in them turned up nothing but gravel and dirt. Others believed they were caused by some kind of volcanic activity. Some think they were created by spawning fish when the area was under water. Spreading plant roots, strange erosion, and various other causes have been suggested.

My favorite theory is the one that says the mounds were deposited by glaciers. Isn't it likely that the glaciers that extended down into the area were carrying a load of sand, gravel, and silt? Naturally. Then when the glaciers melted, the debris would heat faster than the ice, causing the material to collect in little pockets on the ice and finally fall to the ground below. Well, perhaps nearly a million little piles on one glacier is pushing credibility somewhat, but it is as good a theory as any other theory.

Most of the mound area is privately owned, and the only way visitors may enter the fields is with prior permission through the botany department of Evergreen State College in Olympia.

The area makes a nice loop trip. We did it by driving from I-5 to Littlerock, then along the western edge of the prairie on Highway 121 to Rochester. This follows the small, sluggish Black River along the low hills on the pretty road. Several times a year this highway is closed to auto traffic for special Bicycle Sundays.

The road ends at Rochester. Turn west on US Highway 12 toward Oakville and about a mile later, turn north (right) on Highway 121 at a sign that says Gate. This narrow road follows the edge of the valley on the west side, then emerges into the prairie at the Weyerhaeuser nursery near the point where the mounds begin.

*Weyerhaeuser
tree nursery
in Mima Mounds area*

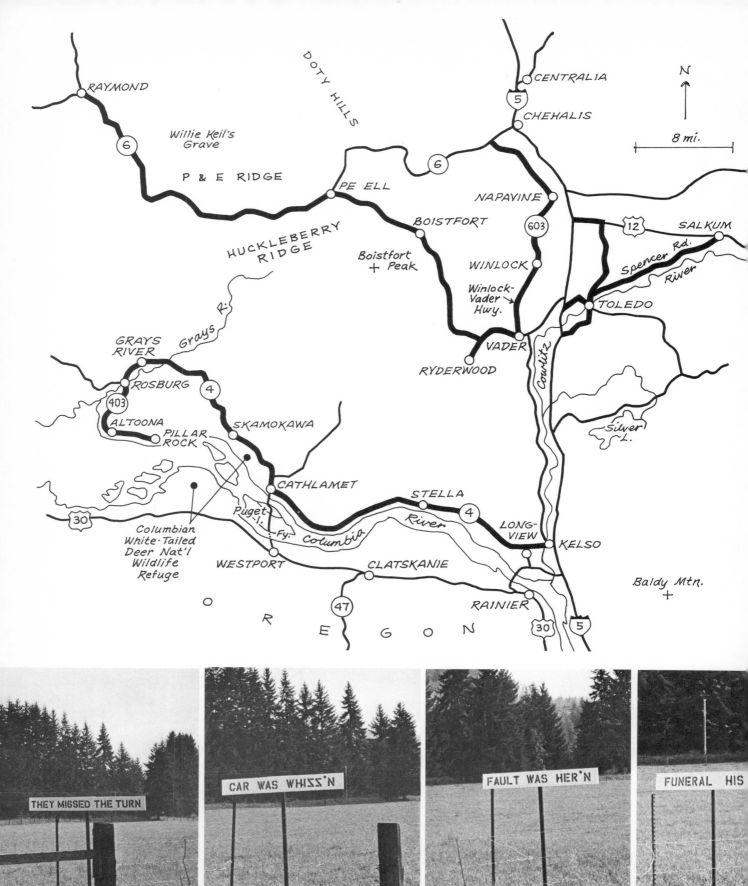

THEY MISSED THE TURN

CAR WAS WHIZZ'N

FAULT WAS HER'N

FUNERAL HIS

WINLOCK, VADER, RYDERWOOD, AND PE ELL

ONE OF THE NICE THINGS about writing this book was that it forced me to go out and look at several areas I had driven near for years but had never visited. Like a healthy person told to get an annual physical checkup, I kept putting it off until I had the time. This book made me have the time.

This tour of some of Lewis County's prettiest farmlands takes you through a group of small towns that have retained a stable population over the years. High school football and basketball teams are cheered with the same intensity as the major leagues, and the local chambers of commerce boast that this town or that one is the home of the Bobcats or whatever the high school team happens to be called.

We started the trip by leaving Interstate 5 at Chehalis and driving west a short distance on Washington Highway 6. We made a turn to the south on Washington 603 toward Napavine and found ourselves driving through the suburbs of Chehalis nearly all the way into Napavine. They were attractive suburbs, to be sure, lining a winding road that climbed up and down the gentle hills; nevertheless it was suburbia.

Things improved from Napavine south toward Winlock. The scenery became more bucolic, with dairy herds grazing on the roll-ing meadows between clumps of fir and hemlock, and we soon found ourselves in Winlock staring at a gigantic egg with an attendant sign calling it the world's largest. No chicken I have ever seen laid that egg, and only a frightening creature from prehistoric periods, or from a very bad dream, could have produced it.

After checking around a bit, we found that the egg was a relic of a promotion dating back to the 1920s, when US Highway 99 was built between Portland and Seattle and towns along the way were asked to construct floats that would travel the entire route as part of the opening ceremonies. Please understand, those of you too young to appreciate all the popular-culture activities of the past, that new highways in those days were major events. It was Big News when a highway was built, unlike today when the construction workers take down the barricades and run for their lives after they complete a stretch of Interstate.

At any rate, Winlock was big in the egg business in those days, and the town created a gigantic papier-mâché egg to put on a float, which made a hit in the Highway 99 parade. Flushed with the success of the highway opening, the townspeople got together and built an even larger permanent egg of concrete and erected it on wooden poles on the edge of town with a sign proclaiming Winlock as the egg capital of the world. A bit of exaggeration, perhaps, but nobody minded.

They did mind what happened to the big egg, though. The poles caught a severe case of rot and collapsed, hurling the egg to the ground and breaking it into many pieces. Undaunted, even though Winlock no longer was known for its egg production, the town built a new egg of plastic and put it on a pedestal near the railroad tracks, where it still stands.

When we drove south on the Winlock–Vader Highway, we found a number of ultra-conservative political announcements posted

*Reincarnated
Burma Shave signs*

153

along the highway. I will refrain from quoting them to avoid being accused of not giving all political parties and philosophies equal time. But I won't restrain myself when it comes to the revived Burma Shave signs that were apparently just installed by someone who remembers them as fondly as I do. Here again I am showing my age and sense of humor, but I miss those signs along the highways as much as I miss two-bits-a-gallon gasoline. The photos show one of the two Burma Shave sign series placed on the road southwest of Vader, and here are some all-time favorites from my childhood on two-lane highways:

Within this vale
Of toil and sin
Your head grows bald
But not your chin—use
Burma Shave

If hugging
On highways
Is your sport
Trade in your car
For a davenport

Slow down, Pa
Sakes alive
Ma missed signs
Four
And five

If harmony
Is what you crave
Then get a tuba
Burma Shave

After seeing these resurrected signs between Vader and Ryderwood, I was in a proper state of mind to visit the retirement town of Ryderwood again after several years. Originally it was a logging town owned by the Long-Bell Lumber Company out of Longview. When the forests were logged off in the area, the town no longer had a function and became virtually a ghost town. Then someone had the great idea of turning it into a retirement village. It has been very successful in that capacity, and the last I heard, there was still a waiting list for the small cottages that line either side of the broad main street.

Ryderwood isn't a town for the inactive senior citizen. A newspaper sent me there for a story, and the residents were so busy with their home-repair projects, crafts, and hobbies that we had difficulty getting enough people together for photographs. They simply didn't care if their pictures were in the papers or not. After a few years of dealing with camera hogs, the photographer and I were charmed by the townspeople and wondered why other similar towns weren't turned into retirement villages as well.

From Ryderwood back northwest toward Highway 6 again is some of the prettiest dairy farming land I've ever seen. It seems that almost every farm along the route has won some kind of award, and even in late August the fields were incredibly lush and green. Some of the barns and silos are crowded right up against the paved road, and I had to stop once to let a herd of cows cross in front of me, urged along by a young man wearing hip boots and red flannel shirt.

There is an intersection at the small village of Boistfort with the main road going almost due north back to Highway 6. I took the west turn toward Pe Ell and drove through more of the same quiet, rural scenery, coming out at the town that had started its career as Pierre. The story about the name change is that the local Indians couldn't pronounce the r's in Pierre and it sounded like Pe-ell, so the whites relented and let the town acquire that name through common usage.

From Pe Ell it is a short drive on to Raymond, a logging and sawmill port town on the Chehalis River near Willapa Bay. There is one more town with an unusual name en route. Lebam was named for the founder's daughter, but rather than being totally literal, he spelled it backward. What Mabel thought of this was not recorded.

Washington Sketch:
WILLIE KEIL

WILLIAM KEIL was a Prussian who became a tailor and moved to America. He was also something of an intellectual and became deeply involved in the concept of Christian communism that swept America during the early part of the 19th century. Out of this religious reform movement came many sects, of which only the Mormons survive in large numbers.

Like so many other Americans in the 1840s and 1850s, Keil and his small band were stricken with Oregon fever, and the group of 61 Bethelites left Missouri with a net worth of $31,000, which made them one of the wealthiest groups to migrate westward during the Oregon Trail era.

Willie Keil sign erected by the state parks system

WILLIE KEIL GRAVE

ON THE HILL BEHIND IS THE GRAVE OF WILLIE KEIL, NINETEEN YEAR OLD SON OF DR. WILLIAM KEIL, LEADER OF THE BETHEL COLONY THAT CAME WEST TO SETTLE HERE IN NOVEMBER, 1855.

WILLIE WAS TO HAVE DRIVEN THE LEADING TEAM IN THE WAGON TRAIN WHICH WAS TO LEAVE BETHEL, MISSOURI IN MAY, 1855. FOUR DAYS BEFORE THEIR DEPARTURE WILLIE DIED. BECAUSE OF HIS GREAT DESIRE TO GO WEST WITH THE GROUP, THE DECISION WAS MADE TO TAKE HIS BODY ALONG. IT WAS PLACED IN A LEAD-LINED BOX FILLED WITH ALCOHOL. THE SEALED COFFIN WAS CARRIED IN A WAGON REMODELED AS A HEARSE WHICH LED THE WAGON TRAIN WEST. IN THE EVENING BY LAMP-LIGHT, WILLIE WAS BURIED HERE NOVEMBER 26, 1855.   WASHINGTON STATE PARKS

Keil's 19-year-old son Willie was excited about the prospects of the trip, and when the group finally prepared to leave in the spring of 1855, he had already been hearing of the trek for half of his life.

But tragedy struck. Shortly before their departure, Willie fell ill with malaria. His grieving parents listened to him in his delirium in which he imagined he was at the head of the column going across the plains and mountains. In his lucid moments, he made his parents promise they wouldn't leave him behind.

Poor Willie died before the trip began, and his parents kept their promise. They built a coffin of lead, placed the boy's body inside, and filled it with alcohol and sealed it tightly. Before his death, Willie's father had built a small wagon on which they would carry the ill boy. Now the wagon was rebuilt to become a hearse.

All the way across the West the hearse led the wagon train, as Willie had led it in his delirium. Much of the time the German emigrants sang, and when they met a hostile band of Indians, they were not attacked. After all, when a group is headed by a dead man, the medicine must be potent. The story of this strange procession traveled ahead of it across the prairies by moccasin telegraph, and no Indian bothered the prosperous group. There was one brief incident when Blackfeet Indians, who did not know who the Bethelites were, stole five head of cattle. Some Sioux took the cattle away from the Blackfeet and returned them.

Virtually nothing else of interest happened along the route. There were a few births along the way, but that was common among emigrant groups. Five months and one week after their departure from Bethel, Missouri, they arrived at their goal of Willapa Bay, Washington. On November 26, 1855, Willie Keil was finally buried, two miles east of the present town of Raymond.

But the Bethelites' travels weren't over. Willapa Bay was too remote for their liking. They were Christian communists and they were businessmen. William Keil went searching for a better home, and found it a few miles south of Portland. He founded a town and named it for his daughter, Aurora. The community prospered, and whenever the Keil family had an opportunity, they visited the grave of their son near Willapa Bay. It is now protected by the state parks system.

TOLEDO LOOP

SOMETIMES after driving on Interstate 5 between Seattle and Portland, I get the urge to pull off on an old-fashioned two-lane highway that is crooked and slow and where traffic is likely to be a tractor pulling a hayrake. Since Interstate driving can be as boring as watching paint dry, such short side trips are often a matter of personal safety.

If the weather is clear, you'll catch glimpses of Mount Rainier and Mount St. Helens from the freeway, and the Toledo side trip will offer a further tonic for the eyes. This small, picturesque town has excellent views of the two mountains, with an old barn advertising a medicine for weak women thrown in as a bonus.

Actually, there are three choices to make on your short trip. You can turn east off Interstate 5 at US Highway 12 and two miles later turn south toward Toledo, or you can go about 12 miles to Salkum and turn south on Spencer Road.

The third choice is limited to northbound traffic on Interstate 5. Take the Toledo exit into town, keep left at all intersections, and you'll soon be back on the freeway.

Too little has been made of Toledo's history. Other states involved in the great migration over the Oregon Trail have taken the events much more seriously than Washington. We are often reminded in publications of the importance of the migration in Oregon and the other states, but for some reason very little is written about how the emigrants got themselves from the Columbia River to Puget Sound. Many emigrants traveled by steamboat down the Columbia to what is now the twin cities of Longview and Kelso, but at the time called Monticello. Then they rode steamboats up the Cowlitz River as far as riverboats could travel, to Cowlitz Landing. The Roman Catholic Cowlitz Mission was established nearby in 1839, and in 1851 a convention was held there to petition Congress for creation of what became Washington Territory.

Cowlitz Landing was soon replaced by a town a short distance up the Cowlitz, which was named Toledo in honor of a steamboat of the same name that served the river for many years.

Until the area was penetrated by railroads, beginning in 1873, emigrants went overland from Cowlitz Landing to Olympia, where they could ride steamboats to Puget Sound settlements and continue up the major rivers in smaller boats.

Several years ago I took a photo of a barn south of Toledo with the medicine advertisement painted all over three sides. I was afraid the barn had been repainted, or that it had collapsed as so many of my favorite barns have over the years. But it is still there on the main road back to the freeway that goes across the Cowlitz River near an old warehouse-style building that dates back to the steamboat days. Just south of the bridge, turn west and the road joins the freeway on the north bank of the Cowlitz River.

The other road, Washington 505, continues south from Toledo. It joins Washington Highway 504, the Mount St. Helens–Spirit Lake Road, a few miles east of Toutle. On a clear day this is a beautiful drive, too, and you can see Mount St. Helens reflected on the calm waters of Silver Lake between the 504–505 intersection and Interstate 5.

Historical medicine advertisement near Toledo

WASHINGTON HIGHWAY 4

Above:
Skamokawa

Facing page:
Barn near Monroe

IF YOU HAVE EVER DRIVEN this stretch of highway, from Kelso–Longview to the Long Beach Peninsula, you will wonder why I have included it in the backroad category. During the busy tourist season the two-lane highway is clogged with campers and trailers, and the highway hasn't been improved to the point that it has a slow-traffic lane on all hills and turnouts for slow vehicles to let the rest of the traffic roar along.

But this route, locally called the Ocean Beach Highway, is one of the prettiest and most varied in Western Washington. As you leave Longview headed west you pass numerous sloughs off the Columbia River where thousands if not millions of logs are stored in the calm water while waiting their turn at the mills of Longview. Some of the logs remain there so long that weeds and willow trees grow on them.

Just beyond these sloughs is the one- or two-building town of Stella, which for years had a rickety old building with a Clabber Girl baking soda sign on it. But the last time I drove past, the building was getting weaker and weaker in the knees and looked like a tired old horse trying to lie down without

simply flopping over. The baking soda sign wasn't in sight, perhaps the victim of an artifact hunter.

One of the premier experiences of driving the highway along the Columbia River is to take off on a foggy morning and suddenly see an oceangoing freighter loom up out of the fog. This is a major shipping lane with cargo ships from all over the world calling on Longview, Kalama, and Portland. Their presence and the strong tidal flow that stops and reverses the flow of the river twice daily give the area a maritime flavor.

We lived in Longview several years ago and became so well acquainted with the highway that I even had a pet tree beside the pavement, which you will agree is much better than a pet rock. I guess. This particular tree, a vine maple, was something like a puppy. It was pretty while it was young and I enjoyed watching it change shape and color with the seasons. But on my last trip it was just another vine maple about to force its way into the power lines overhead.

After following the river only a few feet above the water, the highway takes a climbing turn away from the river just outside

Cathlamet. There is no actual turnout built there, but there is room to pull over and park to look down on Puget Island, the only inhabited island in the Columbia River. The island is flat and ringed with high dikes, which double as roads, and a few sloughs poke back into the island.

You can drive onto the island from the main street of Cathlamet, a tiny and charming town populated by fishermen, loggers, and retired people. The bridge arches high above a channel and deposits you on the small Little Island, also ringed with a dike road. A short bridge puts you on Puget Island and amid the dairy farms that constitute the major portion of the land. The area was settled by Scandinavians and Swiss, the former primarily fishermen and the latter farmers.

The sloughs that poke back into the island are used mainly as parking strips for the gillnet fishing boats, and this is one place in the state where you will see two- and three-boat garages behind the houses. I assume that the Corps of Engineers has completed its dike repair by now. The roads, except the main road straight across the island to the ferry dock, were composed of boulders from the size of a cake upward, and I was so worried about getting back to the main road that I didn't stop once: I was afraid I'd hear that unmistakable hissing of a ruined tire.

The island is served by a small ferry that runs back and forth between the Oregon shore and the south side of Puget Island. The fare is 50 cents per car, and the trip reminds you of jungle river movies because it heads back into a long, narrow, and curving slough before landing in Oregon near Wauna.

A short distance beyond Cathlamet, just after you cross the Elochoman River, is the eastern end of the relatively new Columbian White-Tailed Deer National Wildlife Refuge, which takes in 5,200 acres of land between Highway 4 and the Columbia River, plus some of the low-lying islands out in the river. The Columbian white-tail is a subspecies of the regular white-tailed deer and was on the endangered species list before the refuge was established. The deer are much like their slightly larger cousins, and sometimes in the early morning and evening you can see them out in the pastures grazing beside the dairy cattle that share the refuge.

The road leading through the refuge is alternately marked Steamboat Slough and Wildlife Refuge. At any rate, it is the first road west of Cathlamet that leads toward the river. It winds around atop a dike beside the slough and comes out in Skamokawa, one of the prettiest towns along the river. Skamokawa is derived from an Indian word or words for "smoke on the water," their descriptive name for the frequent fog in the area that hugs the three creeks that merge and enter the Columbia there. Originally it was called "Little Venice" by some settlers, due to its canal-like stream and the houses that line its banks back away from the river.

Skamokawa was a popular stopping place during the steamboat era on the Columbia, and one or two of the buildings from that era still stand out over the calm backwaters.

After Skamokawa, the highway swings back inland and into the forest to go over KM Hill, which is less than a thousand feet high but high enough to collect deep snow in the winter and create driving problems. Then it drops back down nearly to sea level and passes through the small town of Grays River, which is just above the banks of the river by the same name.

Just before you reach the town, look south of the road and you will see the last covered bridge in use in the whole state. After several close brushes with disaster, both from floods and neglect, the bridge has been saved under the National Historic Site designation. You can cross it, turn right, and drive through the dairy farming area on into Grays River.

From here it is only a short distance to the store-and-gas-pump town of Rosburg, which has a side trip worth its own chapter. The rest of the trip to the Long Beach peninsula is mostly inland, away from the river.

Facing page:
Deception Pass bridge

ROSBURG, ALTOONA, AND PILLAR ROCK

NO ROAD led to Altoona and Pillar Rock until well after World War II, even though many families, primarily Finnish emigrants, lived along Grays River, which empties into the Columbia, forming a large bay nearby. Others lived up Crooked Creek in a place called Eden Valley, and still others built homes and small orchards on the bluffs along the Columbia River overlooking the towns of Altoona and Pillar Rock.

These were the salmon-cannery towns built out over the river on piling, quite tall piling because the sea is so close that the tidal surge raises and lowers the river several feet twice daily. The first salmon cannery on the river—and in the entire world, some claim—was built only a few miles upstream at Eagle Cliff in 1865. Soon the entire lower river was dotted with salmon canneries, because the river and its tributaries were choked with spawning salmon every summer and fall.

The early canneries were crude operations, indeed. Almost all work had to be done by hand, and the owners found the cheap labor they required among the Chinese workers imported to this country to build the railroads and can the salmon. Downstream from Altoona about 12 miles are several rows of piling out in the river where the town of Knappton once stood. Here the Chinese laborers were first brought and processed. A quarantine building that only recently disintegrated into the river was the first place these laborers were brought. They were kept there several days to see if any contagious diseases broke out among them. If they remained healthy, they were sent to the various canneries along the river. Should any of the Chinese show enough ambition to attempt becoming salmon fishermen themselves, the penalty was severe, and Caucasian fishermen were not scolded unduly for murdering them.

By the turn of this century, automation was taking over the laborers' cannery work, except for cleaning the fish and moving the crates around. The machine that considerably speeded up the canning process was called the Iron Chink, and is still called that in salmon-canning circles.

Until the road was built in the late 1940s,

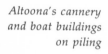

Altoona's cannery and boat buildings on piling

the only way to get in and out of Altoona and Pillar Rock was by water. Those going shopping downriver at Astoria, Oregon, either went in the family boat or caught one of the steamers that went up and down the river between Astoria and Portland. Many fishermen—for fishing is what nearly everyone did for a living then—did not have powered boats, and longtime residents still speak wistfully of the beauty of the sailboats coming home as the tide ebbed, their triangular sails catching the last light of day.

This has all changed, like nearly everything else. Washington Highway 403 was built from the store-and-post office town of Rosburg on Washington Highway 4. It swoops up over a bridge across Grays River, then follows Grays River around curves and cuts inland after a few miles to go over a low set of hills, then again descends to the river at the Crooked Creek bridge. Grays Bay widens and is more than a mile across. The road follows the north bank until it reaches the Columbia River, then turns east upriver toward Altoona.

Along the road are a few places where you can turn off and watch the river traffic—oceangoing ships coming down from Portland, Kalama, and Longview, fishing boats, tugs towing barges or log booms, and an occasional pleasure craft. The Columbia is some four miles across here, dotted with low sandy islands, and the air has a tangy, salty flavor.

You will see Altoona a short distance before you get to it, time enough to pull over and observe this decaying town that really should be preserved as a museum, as should its neighbor, Pillar Rock.

Each time we visit the two towns, a little more of each has fallen down into the Columbia. These are the last of the salmon-cannery towns along the river.

Altoona has, or recently had, very large buildings out over the river including the cannery buildings, a general store, several buildings to store boats and nets and the like. Perched on the bluff across the road are

a number of small frame houses occupied by fishermen, loggers, and some members of the so-called alternative society who want peace and quiet.

Pillar Rock is about three miles farther along the road, which now is gravel, and the drive along the bluffs and down in creek valleys is a pretty one. There is a large sandy beach where river dredges dumped their spoils, and an occasional carpenter-Gothic home built when salmon fishing was a lucrative occupation.

Pillar Rock is in some ways a duplicate of Altoona, and was named for a basalt pinnacle standing a few yards offshore. The first mention of the pinnacle was by Lieutenant William Broughton, who noted it in his journals on October 25, 1792. Broughton was sent up the Columbia River by Captain George Vancouver and he went as far as the confluence of the Willamette River, where the Hudson's Bay Company in 1825 established Fort Vancouver. En route Broughton followed that European explorer's penchant for naming everything that didn't move, and immortalized Lieutenant Peter Puget again by naming a large island in the river in his honor. Captain Vancouver had already named Puget Sound for him, which leads historians to believe Puget was a popular fellow.

When Lewis and Clark came through in the autumn of 1805, they commented on the pinnacle's presence, and in 1841 Lieutenant Charles Wilkes added his impressions and even climbed it. He said it was composed of conglomerate "pudding" stone, and had difficulty climbing it because the pudding kept crumbling beneath his feet.

Later the Hudson's Bay Company had a salmon salting plant there, and by 1878 a commercial salmon cannery was in operation. By the 1890s, there were 39 canneries on the river and some 1,000 boats fishing the river.

Does this historic pinnacle have a historical marker nearby to explain its significance? Of course not. A navigational beacon is perched on its crest.

163

Washington Sketch:
INVITATION TO A HANGING

EVERY EXECUTION is a tragedy, but everyone involved in the execution of Lum You on Friday, January 31, 1902, in South Bend, then the county seat of Pacific County, believed it was an unusually tragic event. This is all the more strange because Lum You was Chinese, and at that time Chinese cannery and farm workers were treated as poorly as black slaves were treated in the South. So intense was the general dislike of all Chinese that any cannery worker caught fishing on his own could be shot with a minimum of questions asked.

However, Lum You had gained a great deal of respect in the white community. He was friendly without being fawning. He was something of a dandy and liked to wear immaculate clothing cut in the English style. He wore jade bracelets, a large gold watch, and a very long queue that, on special occasions, was braided with fine China silk with an ornate tassel.

Lum You was the agent between workers and employers and thus became acquainted with many members of the white community. One member he dealt with briefly was the South Bend police chief Marion Egbert, to whom he had gone when he had been threatened by another Chinese man. The policeman told him to settle it himself; he believed that the Chinese had their own set of laws and that they should settle all disputes among themselves.

In August, 1901, a white man with the reputation of a bully by the name of Oscar Bloom began picking on Lum You. He bumped into him on the streets, sending the smaller man into the gutter, tipped over his chair and knocked the cards out of his hands during a card game. Bloom singled the Chinese out for his bullying tactics and no white man would come to Lum You's aid.

One night Bloom attacked Lum You and took all his valuables and more than $40 in cash. Lum You went to his room and put one bullet in his pistol and went back to the scene of the attack and shot Bloom, who lived long enough to make a statement to the police that, not surprisingly, wasn't entirely accurate.

Lum You was tried for murder in October and at first the jury voted 11–1 for acquittal. But one man, who didn't like Chinese, held out and wore the others down until they voted for conviction under the assumption that Lum You would receive a light sentence, considering the circumstances. But the judge ordered him hanged, to the community's shock and disbelief.

Yet the white community, including the police themselves, made every effort to save Lum You's life. The cell door was never locked and they even told Lum You to escape. But the confused man was afraid to. He thought he might be deported to China in disgrace, where he would be beheaded and separated from his sacred queue, which would prevent him from entering heaven. However, he did disappear once, to everyone's relief, and the community went through the motions of offering a $200 reward for his capture, hoping nobody would catch him. They thought the matter was closed. However, when Lum You heard of the reward he returned to jail rather than cause trouble or lose face.

So the county workers went about building a scaffold over a ventilator opening in the floor of the courthouse, operated by a maze of ropes that required four men to operate them without knowing which man's rope would open the trapdoor.

It was a custom of the time to issue invitations to executions, and to order some young boys to witness them as a deterrent to crime. Attending public hangings was, to be frank, a form of entertainment, and some 500 invitations to Lum You's hanging were printed.

When Lum You was brought into the execution chamber, he spoke politely to all his friends, asking them to wish him luck. When the hood was placed over his head, he told them, "Kill me good."

A deputy provided a grave site on his property for Lum You, and for years afterward Chinese people visited the grave and made offerings to Lum You's spirit. The deputy, Z. B. Brown, built a wrought-iron enclosure around the grave for protection from vandals and it still stands.

BATTLE GROUND, YACOLT, AND AMBOY

THE YACOLT BURN, Washington's worst forest fire; legends of the ape men called Sasquatches or Big Foot; and D. B. Cooper, the skydiving skyjacker, are all part of the folklore in this upper corner of Lewis County. This tour leads you through some of the prettiest foothills in the Cascades, along rivers that are sunken into narrow gorges, and down narrow roads that seem to have been tunneled through the timber.

From Vancouver, take Washington Highway 500 northeast out of town toward Battle Ground, and before you've left the suburbs behind, you'll be passing ramshackle old store buildings and rich farmlands on both sides of the road. Vancouver is one of the fastest-growing cities in Washington as more and more people live in Washington and work in Portland, so you'll see the outskirts of Vancouver gradually taking over the farmland and surrounding small towns.

This area was very important to the development of the Pacific Northwest in the middle of the 19th century due to the presence of the Hudson's Bay post at Fort Vancouver, and especially due to its chief factor, Dr. John McLoughlin. The British and Hudson's Bay executives thought poorly of McLoughlin's policy of aiding newcomers from the United States who were settling in the disputed Oregon Territory. McLoughlin's assistance was directly responsible for Americans displacing the British in what came to be the US Northwest.

Before you start this backroad venture, you should consider stopping by the Fort Vancouver National Historic Site in the heart of Vancouver. The National Park Service has rebuilt the palisades around the fort, the single tower from which only friendly cannon fire was heard as salutes to welcome arriving dignitaries, the chief factor's residence, and a scattering of other buildings. On a hill overlooking the fort is the interpretative center that tells the story of the fort, pointing out that although it was called a fort, no battles were ever fought there.

As you leave Vancouver on the tour, it is best to follow markers indicating Battle Ground; road signs are no more plentiful here than in any other part of the state. Battle Ground is a pleasant small town that is rapidly becoming a center for vineyards as well as the usual row crops and grain.

From Battle Ground, follow the road signs along County Road No. 7 toward Battle

165

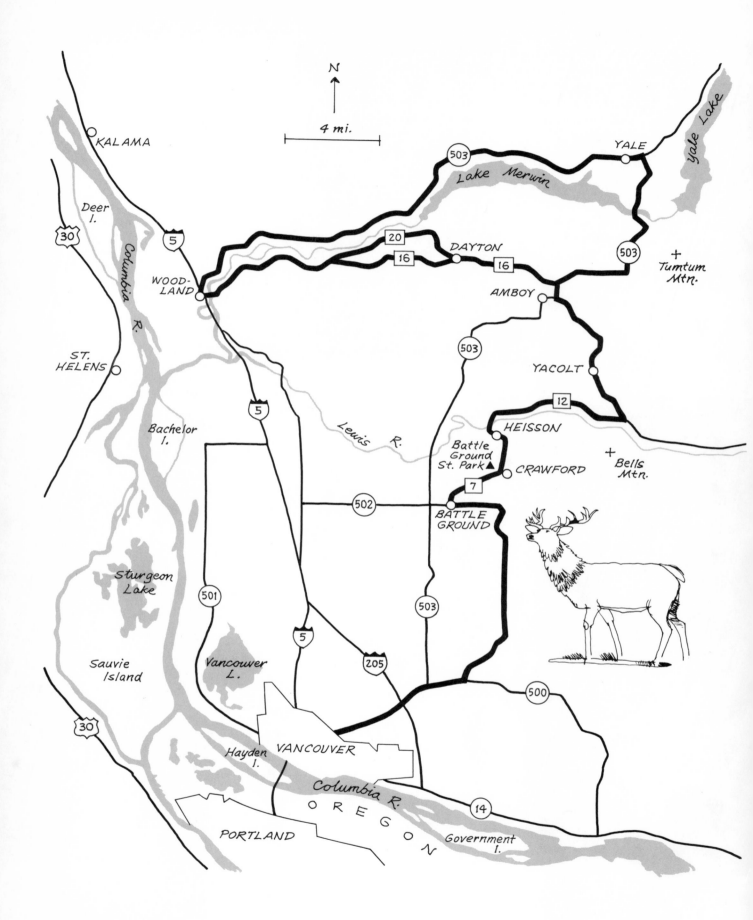

N

4 mi.

KALAMA

Deer I.

30

Columbia R.

5

WOOD-LAND

ST. HELENS

Bachelor I.

Sturgeon Lake

501

Sauvie Island

30

Vancouver L.

5

Hayden I.

PORTLAND

VANCOUVER

205

502

Lewis R.

503

Battle Ground St. Park

7

CRAWFORD

BATTLE GROUND

503

500

Columbia R.

14

Government I.

OREGON

HEISSON

12

Bells Mtn.

YACOLT

503

AMBOY

503

16

DAYTON

16

20

Lake Merwin

503

YALE

503

Tumtum Mtn.

Yale Lake

Ground State Park. This road takes you to Crawford and Heisson, tiny towns that hardly exist as more than a gathering of small houses. Stay on the main road and quite suddenly it drops down into a canyon with the East Fork of the Lewis River at the bottom. On the downstream side of the bridge you will see several holes, like swallows' nests, worn into the rocks beside the river. These were caused over a period of years, if not centuries, by the interaction of water, of small stones, and the lava that had flowed here from Mount St. Helens a short distance to the north. Apparently a small stone would become lodged in a depression in the soft lava, and as the water washed it back and forth, the stone gradually wore deep pockmarks into the dark lava.

Take a right turn to the east on County Road No. 12, which follows the river a few miles with an occasional view of the narrow canyon. There are two waterfalls along this stretch but a fee must be paid to reach them across private land.

The road, which is paved, turns almost due north and emerges from the canyon onto more farmland, then enters Yacolt, a town with a name shared by one of the Northwest's worst forest fires and certainly the worst in Washington's recorded history.

The conflagration actually was a series of fires that broke out at the same time in September, 1902, and destroyed more than 700,000 acres all the way up and down the Cascades. Since the worst destruction was centered around the Yacolt area, the disaster

North Fork of the Lewis River

became known as the Yacolt Burn. It took the lives of 35 people before it finally burned itself out. It turned Portland dark at noon for several days, and many people thought one of the volcanoes, Mount St. Helens or Mount Adams, had erupted. Some religious groups believed the world was ending. Ironically, though, the town for which it was named was not burned, although the inferno came close enough to Yacolt to scorch the paint off houses.

Over the years the burn area partially reforested itself naturally, but for decades state and federal agencies, plus the owners of privately held forests, have been at work removing the millions of snags and replanting seedlings.

From Yacolt, follow the only paved road north to Amboy. Here you will have a choice of turning right on Washington Highway 503 and going across the Lewis River to Yale, then taking 503 west to Woodland and Interstate 5. This route follows the shores of two major Pacific Power & Light reservoirs and passes several campgrounds and picnic areas. It also leads to a series of logging roads that take you into the Mount St. Helens backcountry, and to a series of lava tubes called Ape Caves. For this trip, we stuck to the

backroads and followed County Road No. 16 west.

Now you are in D. B. Cooper country. Cooper was the name given by a well-dressed gentleman who boarded a Northwest Orient Airline Boeing 727 one evening in 1972. Once aboard, he demanded $200,000 and a parachute. When the money and parachute were delivered, the plane was ordered on a specific route south from Seattle. Somewhere over northern Lewis County, Cooper bailed out into the dark night and hasn't been heard from since. Most locals expect to find his skeleton dangling from parachute straps in the dense forest; others believe he landed safely and went back to living his normal life with the money hidden somewhere.

Eight miles along this road, west of Amboy, is the Old Cedar Creek Grist Mill, a beautiful old mill with water wheel that has been placed on the National Register of Historic Sites. The signs leading to it are a sometime thing, and we finally had to give up and ask at one of the nearby farmhouses for directions. Since the mill is not staffed, this casual approach to attracting visitors has the effect of protecting it from overuse and vandalism.

At Dayton we decided to swing back to the river and took County Road 20 down toward the river, driving through some deep canyons in what my son called the twilight zone. The road has turnouts to the Lewis River just below the dam that creates Lake Merwin. But be advised that the river level is controlled entirely by the dam and can fluctuate several feet in a matter of minutes depending on the power needs at the dam.

This route is a good loop trip, and we saw a portion of County Road 16 twice. It was fortunate we did because not far from the grist mill is a great view of Mount St. Helens across the wheat fields that slope down toward the river.

County Road 16 follows the Lewis River on into Woodland, where you can rejoin Interstate 5, if you must.

Pockmarked lava on the North Fork of the Lewis River

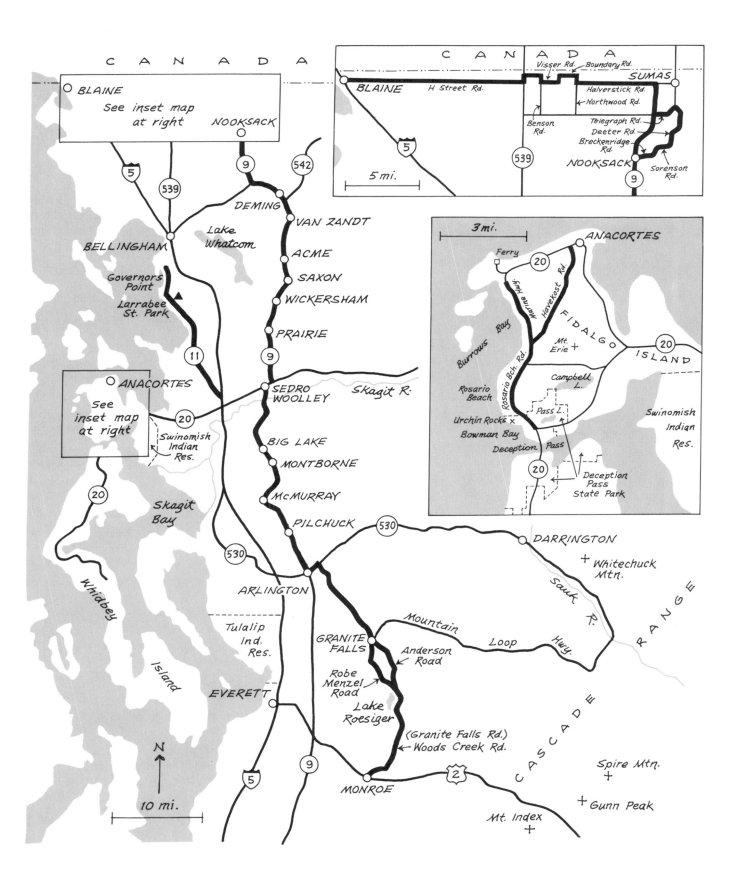

MONROE, GRANITE FALLS, AND ARLINGTON

Shady road between Arlington and Granite Falls

THIS PRETTY ROAD begins in Monroe at Woods Creek Road, which turns north off US Highway 2 and follows the creek valley north out of town. It is one of those old-fashioned roads that are narrow, hilly, and often go through thick trees that form a canopy overhead. It passes small farms, hayfields, and occasional lakes.

Locals call it the Granite Falls Road because that is where it goes, but getting there makes a very interesting drive. Midweek is a better time to take the trip because of the weekend traffic to and from Lake Roesiger, where many families have cabins and boats. Their teenagers zoom to and from the lake, making some curves more exciting for you than others. But ordinarily you can cruise along this road at 35 miles an hour and never get in the way.

This is foothill topography, and very few of the farms are flat. You will see hayfields rolling upward against the timbered slopes, picturesque barns, and occasional stands of fir and hemlock lining the highway and filtering the sunlight to create dappled patterns on the road.

Just north of Lake Roesiger is an intersection with a road heading back toward Lake Stevens and Everett. You can stick with the main road, which by now has become Anderson Road, or you can turn west toward Lake Stevens, go less than a mile, and turn north

on Robe Menzel Road. Either route will get you to Granite Falls.

It is always pleasant to come upon a town like Granite Falls. Suddenly you drive out of the countryside and find yourself in the middle of town. There are no suburbs, no rows of junkyards and neon signs, and usually no traffic lights. The transition from country to town is immediate.

Granite Falls is the first town on the famous Mountain Loop Highway, which cuts back into the Cascades. To follow it, turn right on the main street and follow the signs toward the falls of the Stillaguamish River for which the town was named. To continue on north toward Arlington, or back to Lake Stevens, Marysville, and Everett, turn left at the main street.

The road to Arlington is a bit tricky, not because it isn't properly signed but because you make two right turns so close together that it seems you've doubled back toward Granite Falls. But the road straightens itself out and heads up the Jordan Valley with the South Fork of the Stillaguamish wandering along the same route to join the North Fork in Arlington.

In Arlington you are back within shouting distance of Interstate 5, or you can head east on Washington Highway 530, which is the northern portion of the Mountain Loop Highway.

WASHINGTON HIGHWAY 9

EARLIER I lamented the passing of those highways we used to take that got us there but took a little more time to do it. Washington Highway 9 is such a road, and it is one of the most pleasant means of getting from the Seattle area to the Canadian border. It dips and turns and climbs and swerves. It passes pleasant farm scenes, lakes, mailboxes, small towns, and goes from low hills to the flat Nooksack Valley plain up against the Canadian border.

Highway 9 probably starts in the Seattle suburb of Woodinville, but it first shows on the map as a turn off Washington Highway 522 between Woodinville and Monroe. Since suburbia engulfs it most of the way to Arlington, don't feel you've missed much if you decide to catch it at Arlington. On our journey, there was no directional sign in Arlington pointing to Highway 9. Finding the route is relatively simple though, since Highway 9 brushes the edge of Arlington and intersects the main east-west highway into town, Washington 530.

From Arlington all the way to Sumas on the Canadian border, the road passes pastoral instead of urban scenery. It goes through places such as Pilchuck, McMurray, Montborne, Big Lake, Prairie, Wickersham, Saxon, Acme, Van Zandt, and a few other spots on the map that are communities rather than towns. Nearly all the way it parallels Interstate 5 with less than ten miles between the two, but in terms of scenery and driving attitudes, they seem 50 years apart.

After you leave Arlington, the only town of substantial size you will go through before the border area is Sedro Woolley, site of headquarters for North Cascades National Park. And don't expect a lot of parks to camp in; the road is not a recreational thoroughfare and all the places for picnic lunches or overnight stays are off to the side somewhere.

When you reach Deming, the highway briefly joins Washington Highway 542. Just when you think you're back on the busy highways for good, you reach a junction that sends you north again on Highway 9 and into Nooksack. This pleasant small town, with a city park on the north edge beside a railroad spur, has the stores and service stations you've been looking for since leaving Sedro Woolley, and the dairy-farm scenery— and aromas—you expected to find in the Nooksack Valley.

The whole valley is dotted with well-kept dairy farms and two- and three-silo barns. There are thousands of acres of hayfields and a variety of berry farms and bulb nurseries.

A good side trip through the valley is to turn right (east) from Nooksack on Breckenridge Road just south of the city park. The road runs into Sorenson Road, which leads to Deeter Road, then into Telegraph Road, which deposits you safely in Sumas. In the meantime, you've swung around against the low hills that ring the Nooksack Valley and beneath Haystack and Sugarloaf Hills and through some beautiful farmland.

The main industry in Sumas appears to be farming and border crossing. The crossing here isn't nearly as busy as that on Interstate 5 to the west in Blaine, and there are a number of shops and stores along Sumas's main street where you can take a break before or after going through customs.

Cattle grazing along Washington 9

BORDER PATROL

COUNTRIES TAKE very few things more seriously than their boundaries. Wars are fought over them, fantastic sums of money are spent patrolling them, and it seems some country is always complaining that its neighbor is elbowing into its territory.

It is refreshing to travel along the US–Canadian border and see how countries really should conduct themselves at their frontiers. For a look at this study in peaceful coexistence, start the trip in Sumas, the last town on Washington Highway 9 before entering Canada.

Halverstick Road heads west off Highway 9 just outside Sumas and goes between dairy and berry farms. At Northwood Road, turn right (north) to Boundary Road, which turns left (west).

Here you will see parallel blacktop roads separated only by a shallow ditch that is no more than two feet deep in places and less than six feet across. That shallow trench is the US–Canadian border. Utility poles are strung down the ditch, and that is all. There are no barbed-wire fences, no armed patrols.

On either side of the roads are farmhouses with mailboxes, and during berry-picking season, you'll probably see "pickers-wanted" signs on both sides of the border.

Boundary Road is reasonably named, and it continues along in its dual fashion for a little more than a mile, then jogs back to the south. About half a mile south you'll come to Visser Road. Take it a mile to its end, turn north on Benson Road, and you'll soon be back on Boundary Road again. This section is a bit less than a mile long, and ends at Washington Highway 539, a border crossing. From here you can enter Canada or take Highway 539 south into Bellingham. A third alternative is to turn west on the first road off Highway 539, H Street Road, which takes you into Blaine after going through a wooded, hilly area with few farms.

When we traveled Boundary Road, two of our children were along and they were intrigued by the whole concept. I stopped for photographs and they jumped out and ran over into Canada, trying to provoke an international incident. If anyone was watching, we didn't see him. Disappointed that no mines exploded and no sirens sounded from watchtowers, the children got back into the car, ready to go where something would happen.

We were told that the boundary area along here was settled by Hollanders, and that several families on either side of the border had intermarried and that they crossed back and forth freely. However, they were close friends of the Border Patrol, and any time someone crossed who didn't seem to belong in the area, the Border Patrol was notified. Apparently children who ran into the middle of the road shouting, "Hello, Canada!" weren't considered a threat.

DECEPTION PASS TO ANACORTES

THE USUAL WAY to visit the state's showcase, Deception Pass State Park, is to follow the main route, Washington Highway 20, across the Deception Pass bridge and onto Whidbey Island. This is a beautiful drive, to be sure. You will see the swirling waters of the passage below, and you can watch boats as they struggle against the current that races through at every tide change.

But a quieter way to visit the park is to turn north on the Rosario Beach Road just after entering the park. The road turns off at the west end of Pass Lake and goes over a low hill before dropping back down again almost to sea level and Rosario Beach.

Rosario Beach is part of Deception Pass State Park, and consists of a beautiful peninsula of beaches and rocks that juts out into the ocean to give you great views of the islands, the shipping, and Canada's Vancouver Island off to the northwest.

Rosario Head has Bowman Bay to the south, with trails leading around it, and Ur-chin Rocks to the north in Rosario Bay. At low tide you can scamper over these rocks and watch the tide pool creatures. This is a favorite spot for scuba divers, and occasionally you'll see commercial fishing boats gathered close to shore following the salmon runs past the head.

The paved road, called Marine Highway, hugs the shoreline around Burrows Bay and joins Washington Highway 20 near the Washington State Ferry terminal where the ferries run out to the San Juan Islands and Victoria, British Columbia. An alternate route, Havekost Road, swings off Marine Highway four miles from the main intersection back at Pass Lake. This takes you past Mount Erie, reached from a well-marked side road to the east. The road climbs to the top of the 1,270-foot mountain, where you will enjoy excellent views across Campbell Lake and Skagit Bay. Continuing along Havekost Road takes you into the small fishing town of Anacortes.

*Fishing fleet
just off
Rosario Beach*

CHUCKANUT DRIVE

Larrabee State Park off Chuckanut Drive

THIS STRETCH of Washington Highway 11 isn't long—only about 12 miles—and the road is old, worn, and given to getting chuckholes in it during the winter that often aren't patched until the following fall. But Chuckanut Drive is a historic and beautiful way to get from Interstate 5 to Bellingham. It was the first scenic highway built in Washington, and is a perennial favorite for people wanting a pleasant afternoon's drive.

The only unfortunate part of the trip is that the route is shared with a railroad that runs along the coast with it, but on a lower level. Now, if they ran steam-powered trains only along this historic route . . .

To reach the drive from Interstate 5, take the Burlington–Deception Pass exit just north of Mount Vernon, then turn north on Highway 11. This takes you across the famed Skagit River Valley, some of the richest farmland in the Northwest. You will know you're on Chuckanut Drive when you hit the first hairpin turn. When the highway reaches Samish Bay, it starts winding around the hillside past an occasional restaurant, then levels off a bit a few feet above water level. The highway shows definite signs of an antique public works program with its walls of stone and concrete, and the ornate bridges that cross gullies. The few turnouts have these same stone walls around them, suitable for sitting on or using in the foreground of photographs.

An excellent picnic stop is Larrabee State Park just south of Governors Point, and around the same general area is a road leading to the crest of Chuckanut Mountain, where more views can be found.

The road ends in Bellingham, and as you enter town you'll pass a number of old but well-cared-for homes. The whole trip will remind you of running boards, cranks, and skinny innertubes.

It is appropriate that this tour be the last in the book because it shows us how much highways, and the public's attitude toward them, have changed within the lifetimes of many people. Which highways would we designate as scenic today? The list would be impossible to make because nearly every highway in the state could qualify according to someone's definition of scenic.

The routes I have chosen for this book were selected not only for a geographical distribution around the state, but also because I have enjoyed traveling each. There are still dozens more to be traveled. I plan to explore them someday soon, and hope you will, too.

Suggestions for Further Reading

If these tours and sketches have whetted your interest in Washington, some of the books listed below may help you broaden your knowledge about the state.

GUIDEBOOKS

Bullard, Oral. *Short Trips and Trails: The Columbia Gorge.* Portland: Touchstone, 1974.

Fish, Byron. *Guidebook to Puget Sound: The Water World that the Indians called Whulge.* Los Angeles: Ward Ritchie, 1973.

Kirk, Ruth. *Exploring the Olympic Peninsula.* Seattle and London: University of Washington Press, 1976.

Krenmayr, Janice. *Footloose Around Puget Sound.* Seattle: The Mountaineers, 1973.

Rayburn, Barbara. *Let's Go! Daytripping In and Around the Palouse.* Pullman, Washington: American Association of University Women, 1974.

Speidel, Bill. *The Wet Side of the Mountains.* Seattle: Nettle Creek, 1974.

Sterling, E. M. *Trips and Trails, 1.* Seattle: The Mountaineers, 1967.

———. *Trips and Trails, 2.* Seattle: The Mountaineers, 1968, 1977.

Sunset Travel Guide to Washington. Menlo Park, California: Lane Publishing, 1978.

Weis, Norman D. *Ghost Towns of the Northwest.* Caldwell, Idaho: Caxton, 1971.

GENERAL

Blankenship, Russell. *And There Were Men.* New York: Knopf, 1942.

Cantwell, Robert. *The Hidden Northwest.* Philadelphia: Lippincott, 1972.

Holbrook, Stewart. *Burning an Empire: The Story of American Forest Fires.* New York: Macmillan, 1943.

———. *Far Corner: A Personal View of the Pacific Northwest.* New York: Macmillan, 1952.

Jones, Nard. *Evergreen Land: A Portrait of the State of Washington.* New York: Dodd Mead, 1947.

Lavender, David. *The Land of Giants: The Drive to the Pacific Northwest, 1750–1950.* New York: Doubleday, 1958.

Satterfield, Archie. *Adventures in Washington.* Mercer Island, Washington: The Writing Works, 1978.

Stevens, Hazard. "The Ascent of Mount Takhoma." *Atlantic Monthly,* November 1876.

———. *The Life of Isaac Ingalls Stevens.* Boston: Houghton Mifflin, 1900.

Waring, Guy. *My Pioneer Past.* Boston: Bruce Humphries, 1936.

Winthrop, Theodore. *The Canoe and the Saddle.* Boston: Ticknor & Fields, 1863.

Works Progress Administration. *Washington: A Guide to the Evergreen State.* Portland: Binfords & Mort, 1940, 1951.

NATURAL HISTORY

Arno, Stephen. *Northwest Trees.* Seattle: The Mountaineers, 1977.

Harris, Stephen L. *Fire and Ice: The Cascade Volcanoes.* Seattle: The Mountaineers, 1976.

Neill, William, and Hepburn, Douglas. *Butterflies Afield in the Pacific Northwest.* Seattle: Pacific Search, 1976.

Rue, Walter. *Weather of the Pacific Coast.* Mercer Island, Washington: The Writing Works, 1978.

Schmoe, Floyd. *A Year in Paradise.* Seattle: The Mountaineers, 1979.

Schwartz, Susan, and Spring, Bob & Ira. *Cascade Companion.* Seattle: Pacific Search, 1976.

HISTORY

Becher, Edmund T. *Spokane Corona*. Spokane: E. T. Becher, 1974.

Binns, Archie. *Northwest Gateway*. Garden City, New York: Doubleday, 1945.

Florin, Lambert. *Victorian West*. Seattle: Superior, 1978.

Holbrook, Stewart. *The Columbia*. New York: Holt, Rinehart & Winston, 1956, 1974.

Majors, Harry M., and McCollum, Richard C. *Monte Cristo Area*. Seattle: Northwest Press, 1977.

Morgan, Murray. *The Last Wilderness*. Seattle and London: University of Washington Press, 1976.

Newell, Gordon, and Wing, Robert C. *Peter Puget*. Seattle: Gray Beard, 1979.

Wood, Robert L. *Across the Olympic Mountains: The Press Expedition, 1889–90*. Seattle and London: University of Washington Press, 1967.

Woodhouse, Philip, and Wood, Robert. *Monte Cristo*. Seattle: The Mountaineers, 1979.

Quiet evening
at low tide
on Rosario Beach